Holy Eros

A Liturgical
Theology of the Body

ADAM G. COOPER

Holy Eros

A Liturgical
Theology of the Body

Foreword by
David W. Fagerberg

 Angelico Press

First published in the USA
by Angelico Press
© Adam G. Cooper, 2014
Foreword © David W. Fagerberg, 2014

For information, address:
Angelico Press
4709 Briar Knoll Dr.
Kettering, OH 45429
angelicopress.com

paperback: 978-1-62138-076-4
eBook: 978-1-62138-077-1

Cover Artwork:
Crucifixion, ink drawing, 2011
by Daniel Mitsui
www.danielmitsui.com
Cover Design: Michael Schrauzer

CONTENTS

Note on Texts
and Translations

Although I have made liberal use of existing English translations of
original sources where they exist, and referenced them in the bibliog-
raphy, I have occasionally modified them according to my own reading of original language editions or by comparison with other
translations. All other translations of non-English texts are my own.

Foreword to

A Liturgical Theology of the Body

G. K. CHESTERTON once quipped about some topic that it would make "one of the best articles he's never written." I also once had an idea that would make one of the best articles I've never taken the time to flesh out. I thought that perhaps every Christological heresy has a potential ecclesiological counterpart. That is, someone could make the same sort of mistake about the Church that heretics in the first centuries made about Christ. For example, a Nestorian ecclesiology might artificially separate the human and divine elements of the Church, thereby failing *Lumen Gentium* 8 when it tells us that "the society structured with hierarchical organs and the Mystical Body of Christ, are not to be considered as two realities." A Monophysite ecclesiology might go wrong by absorbing the human into the divine to the neglect of its real human members, or an Adoptionist ecclesiology might go wrong by focusing upon the human community to the neglect of the divine Christ, making the Church into nothing but a Jesus club with Christ smuggled in as an after-thought.

In line with this idea, I suggest that this rewarding study by Adam Cooper saves us from a *docetic ecclesiology.* Incarnational theology goes wrong when it forgets that Jesus's full humanity requires him to have a true, bodily existence; ecclesiology goes wrong when it thinks the Church is only a spiritual act of God; and liturgical theology goes wrong when it forgets that liturgy is engaged by embodied men and women. This book is "an attempt to understand how the liturgy bodily enacts the truth of our Christian faith, and how that truth in turn is expressed in the structure and bodily actions of Christian worship and the life of Christian discipleship." Cooper intends to explore the embodiment of liturgy.

Suppose we got past an over-spiritualized, docetic view of liturgy, and suppose we admitted that our bodies are involved in our worship. With whom could we make alliance in order to work out a fuller understanding of this idea? There are a variety of other approaches that could be attentive to the presence of bodies in rite. Ritual studies has made this an object of study, so a chapter by Cooper on drama and ritual helps. Philosophers are also sensitive to sign, symbol, and semiotics, so a chapter on metaphysics helps. But finally, the nature of the body that will be most helpful for understanding liturgy will be one that is nuptial. There are dozens of books that could speak about the nature of the body in anthropology or ritual studies, but this work is set apart by using a theology of the body that specially emphasizes the interpersonal potential of the body. John Paul II's nuptial theology of the body recognizes the body's spousal nature.

Christianity operates with an interesting arithmetic. In the Trinity, three persons are still a monotheism. In Christ, two natures are still one person. In marriage, two persons become what John Paul II called a uni-duality. This arithmetic is only possible because of a mutual reciprocity operating in each case. The Church fathers called this *perichoresis*, and first used the word in Christology to affirm that the divine and human natures in Christ did not cancel each other out, but actually together made one person. Then it was applied to the Trinity in order to say that although each person is distinct, they "live towards" each other in a mutual indwelling. It is the nature of love to give itself, to turn outward, turn toward the other and receive the other, and if creatures were to be drawn up into this *circumincession* (the Latin word for it), then they would be participating in the life of God. Such deification is possible by divine initiative and human receptivity, and such is liturgical life. This has led me to define liturgy as *the perichoresis of the Trinity kenotically extended to invite our synergistic ascent into deification*. John Paul II's theology of the body capitalizes on this mutuality in such a way that Cooper can elaborate this definition by exploring how the circulation takes liturgical form.

An observation by Gabriel Marcel seems fittingly applicable here. Marcel wants to overcome a sense of dualism between the subject and the body, and thus recommends avoiding the phrase 'I have a body.' It leaves the impression that there are two things —"me" and "my body"—that must be artificially connected. Some gain is made by saying 'I am a body,' but even if we no longer use a possessive term, the same impression still remains. So ultimately Marcel suggests that we say 'I am bodily.' The way in which I am is bodily. Cooper suggests in this book that the *Church is bodily.* The way in which we liturgize is bodily. The liturgy is an embodied activity. "Through her eucharist in particular the Church is effectively constituted as the Church, a subject whose 'I' is Christ himself."

There is foot traffic going both directions across the bridge that Cooper constructs. In the one direction, liturgy is used to better understand a theology of the body. Using algebraic brackets, the book is a [*liturgical*] [*theology of the body*]. However it is that angels mediate interpersonal realities, human beings do so bodily. This makes theology "fundamentally a doxological, liturgical and thereby *physical* activity. It enables participation in the intimate life of the holy Trinity, not just anyhow, but by very concrete, tangible, interpersonal means: crossing, kneeling, standing, hearing, speaking, singing, embracing, eating, drinking, bowing." Liturgical theology is *theologia prima* because it is the experience of God upon which some academics might later reflect (*theologia secunda*). In the other direction, the theology of the body is used to better understand liturgical theology. The book is a [*liturgical theology*] [*of the body*]. A deeper appreciation of liturgical theology can be derived from John Paul II's suggestion that human beings have been inscribed by God with a nuptial or spousal structure and meaning. Since liturgy is the action of the bride of Christ, and since love is interpersonal and relational, a nuptial theology of the body is in the best position to help us appreciate the mystery that occurs in liturgy.

Many of the Church fathers imagined what a surprise the risen and ascending body of Jesus must have been to the angels in heaven. He doesn't look the same as when he left. Irenaeus writes, "Seeing him approach, the lower angels cried out to those who were above them, 'Open your gates; rise up, ye gates of eternity; the King of Glory will enter.' And when the angels from above asked in their astonishment, 'Who is He?' those who saw Him cried out anew, 'It is the Lord, strong and mighty. It is the King of Glory.'" Gregory of Nyssa explains the source of their confusion. "They do not recognize Him because he has put on the poor tunic of our nature and because His garments were dyed crimson in the winepress of human evils." The angels' puzzled question is on our lips, too: Who is this One who comes into our midst at every liturgy?

The thoroughness of Christ's incarnation makes us hesitate because we cannot fully believe it. Is his incarnation really so complete? Are we wrong to think that spiritual life must be incorporeal? Could an embodied act really be a divine action? Are we truly engaged in eternal matters if we conduct them bodily? Our doctrine of the Church can scarcely accommodate a God of such radical kenosis that he became truly man, and that even now he indwells bodies as temples. Yet that is what we must understand if we are to do liturgical theology. When God speaks, he acts; when the Church-as-theologian replies, she replies by act: embodied liturgical theology.

DAVID W. FAGERBERG
University of Notre Dame

Introduction

What is a Liturgical Theology of the Body?

BLESSED JOHN PAUL II's catecheses on human love in the divine plan will surely be remembered for many generations to come as a superlative contribution to the long tradition of Christian theologizing about the body and sexuality.[1] Taking the teaching of Jesus in Matthew's Gospel as their starting point and structuring guide, they lead us into a deep and prolonged meditative engagement with the word of God expressed in holy Scripture through the dual lens of human experience and authoritative Christian teaching. Although the catecheses are often dense and difficult to read, understanding can be assisted if it is remembered that the Pope's theology of the body is essentially a big Bible study, a mapping out of human sexuality from a three-stage developmental perspective consisting of God's original design, our fallen historical situation, and the new possibilities rendered actual and accessible in the redeemed and Spirit-filled body of Christ.

This little book is also a theology of the body. Its special point of focus and structuring guide is the liturgy, the public worship of the Church. It is an attempt to understand how the liturgy bodily enacts the truth of our Christian faith, and how that truth in turn is expressed in the structure and bodily actions of Christian worship and the life of Christian discipleship.

Even though this book is not meant to be an exposition of John Paul II's teaching as such, nor a guide to its interpretation, a number of deep connections between the theology of the body and the liturgy are suggested by the Pope in the course of his

---

1 John Paul II, *Man and Woman He Created Them: A Theology of the Body*, trans. Michael Waldstein (Boston: Pauline, 2006). Hereafter I shall refer to this work as TOB followed by relevant page number/s.

catecheses. According to his theology of the body, human beings are understood as having been inscribed by God with nuptial or "spousal" structure and meaning. This does not mean that all people are meant to become married, still less that a person is incomplete without sexual experience. Rather, it means that the fact of sexual difference and affective reciprocity stands as a created sign pointing to the even greater fact that we are created for communion with God. Marriage is not just one of the Church's seven sacraments, but is in some sense the sacrament of all sacraments, because it contains and reflects the basic meaning and purpose of every sacramental action: to effect between God and human beings an intimate, transformative, and fruitful communion. This is what John Paul means by "the language of the body." Precisely in its sexual difference, the human body "speaks" something about the shape of our God-given vocation to find fulfilment beyond ourselves, in a gift of self that leads to a deifying communion of persons.

These are not entirely novel ideas. The tradition of thinking "nuptially" about our relationship with God goes right back through many of the greatest theologians and mystics of Christian history to the Israelite prophets. What John Paul II does is extend and deepen this insight with special reference to the concrete reality of bodily sexual specificity, interpreting this reality by means of a range of resources drawn from theology, contemporary philosophy, and human experience. Following Christ's appeal to the Creator's words and deeds from "the beginning" (Mt. 19:4), John Paul wants us above all to listen to the language of creation, the language inscribed by God into sexual difference, so that we may authentically discern and live its redeemed and sanctified form.

This approach enables him at some points to draw a close connection between bodily marital union and Christian worship. In Christian marriage, the language of the body becomes "the language of the liturgy," that is, pregnant with mystery, holiness, and spirit. To celebrate a sacramental marriage is to express in liturgical language "an interpersonal event full of intense personal content." When married couples, led by the Holy Spirit, honour and revere one another out of reverence for Christ, their love-making, along with their whole conjugal life, "in some sense becomes liturgy."[2]

There are other connections to be made between the theology of the body and the liturgy. One lies in the fact that Christian worship functions as the matrix in which the body of Christ is manifested on the stage of history in all its living color. In the wonderfully simple image suggested by Sofia Cavalletti, worship is a kind of "breathing" of the body of Christ: it is the Christian community's most native, animating action, without which it cannot live.[3]

Yet another, more intricate connection between the theology of the body and the liturgy lies in the meaning of the word "theology" itself. From pre-Christian times the term "theology" enjoyed currency as a term referring to any branch of human inquiry whose objects lie beyond the immediacy of sense-perception. Apparently coined by Plato, *theologia* originally meant a kind of mystical vision (*epopteia*) of divine realities, a mode of knowing possessed of quasi-religious qualities. With Aristotle however, *theologia* was made roughly equivalent to metaphysics, one among a number of branches of theoretical philosophy. Without disputing this meaning, early Christian thinkers re-injected a religious sense to the word, though distinguishing it from any mythological connotations. Specifically, they identified the new Christian *theologia* as the highest and only true philosophy, since it involved a real apprehension of the one true God, revealed in his saving works.[4] For them, to study theology was to adopt God's perspective on things, to view reality from his point of view, to embrace all things with a sensitivity and judgement shaped by the perspective of eternity. Later in Christian thought, the term *theologia* increasingly came to express a more specific form of divine knowledge, referring especially to that which is most intimate to God in himself, namely, his intrinsic being as a trinity of persons. *Theologia* thus meant God's activity *ad intra*,

2 TOB, 608–15.

3 Sofia Cavalletti, *Living Liturgy: Elementary Reflections* (Chicago: Liturgy Training Publications, 1998), 27–30.

4 See, for example, Clement of Alexandria, *Stromata* I, 28.

the intimate and eternal relational dynamic of the three divine persons, and so distinct from the sphere of *economia*: God's activity with respect to the orders of creation and redemption. Finally, by the Middle Ages, we see a return to the more "scientific" definition of *theologia* as that branch of human knowledge by which the components of revealed sacred doctrine are systematically arranged.

Among the early Fathers there was, however, yet another meaning of the word *theologia* which tied it much more closely to the doxological and liturgical actions of the worshipping Christian Church. According to this meaning, *theologia* generally meant the praise of God. So we find Cyril of Jerusalem in the fourth century referring to the "Holy, holy, holy" of Isaiah 6, chanted in the eucharistic liturgy, as the *theologia*—"the song of praise" or "confession of God"—handed down to us by the seraphim.[5] By singing it we sanctify ourselves and partake in the perpetual heavenly liturgy. Still earlier, Origen of Alexandria had contrasted the *theologein* of Christian prayer to the babbling of the heretics.[6] To do theology is to join in faith with Christ the Son in his mediating office and reconciling movement towards God the Father. This simultaneously doxological and participatory notion of *theologia* arises again later in the same treatise, where Origen condemns the idolatry of those who have fabricated a Son or Father other than the one "praised" (*theologoumenon*) by the Apostles.[7] Here we discover an understanding of *theologia* as right worship of the one true God, a participation in that communal, ritual activity in which the living Jesus himself, present and active as High Priest and Husband, applies the fruits

---

5 Cyril of Jerusalem, *Mystagogic Catecheses* 5, 6.

6 Origen, *On Prayer* 21, 1.

7 Ibid., 29, 10. "Origen understands theology to be doxological discourse.... It is the mysterious but deliberate entry in the Spirit of a human being—in communion with the saints—into the eternal dialogue of the only-begotten Son with the immortal Father." See Adam G. Cooper, "Christ as Teacher of Theology: Praying the Our Father with Origen and Maximus," in Lorenzo Perrone (ed.), *Origeniana Octava: Origene e la Tradizione Alessandrina* (Leuven: Peters, 2003), 1053–9, at 1053.

4

of his passion to his holy bride, making her a pure offering of devoted love to his Father and hers.

Thus in one, very profound sense, theology is fundamentally a doxological, liturgical and thereby *physical* activity. It enables participation in the intimate life of the holy Trinity, not just anyhow, but by very concrete, tangible, interpersonal means: crossing, kneeling, standing, hearing, speaking, singing, embracing, eating, drinking, bowing. If we can speak of a liturgical theology, we mean not first of all a theology *of the liturgy*, as though the liturgy were a distinct and integral source of theological reflection, perhaps analogous to the role the Church's Scriptures might play in a "biblical" theology. There is of course an appropriate place for this kind of theological discipline. As a dramatic, ever-evolving, culturally specific complex of ritual words and proclamatory deeds, the liturgy forms the proper object of various human sciences. But like all human sciences, this mode of "liturgical theology" is a secondary science: it follows upon a prior, effective mode of knowing that precedes all reflection, indeed, that precedes dogma itself.

Liturgical theology, in the way it is meant in this book, is what some have called the Church's "primary theology." Following the understanding of the Fathers of the Church, it amounts as it were to the affective experience or "suffering" of divine activity. Not passively, like a stone, but receptively, in the form of a beloved's willing personal surrender to the embrace of the lover. As a form of human knowledge or *logos*, this "suffering" is to be distinguished from the processes of discursive reasoning in a manner famously articulated in the axiom first proposed by Aristotle, but later asserted by Dionysius the Areopagite, and assumed by the Church's great mystical doctors: not by learning, but by experiencing (*ou mathon alla pathon*).[8] "To learn" is to proceed towards the apprehension of the truth by rational means, to arrange the data of experience in logical order, to consider, weigh, abstract, discern, and pronounce. "To experience," by contrast, is simply to receive, to be acted upon, rather than to act. It is to "take in" what surpasses the limits of human accomplishment in the form

8 Dionysius the Areopagite, *Divine Names* 2, 9.

of a welcome gift. It is to be formed and shaped by a direct face-to-face encounter with the truth. In short, it is to know God by concretely experiencing him.

In equating liturgical theology with experience I do not mean to exalt subjectivity to the status of a norm and criterion of objective truth. What I am speaking of is a divine-human encounter that precedes all human judgement, even if that judgement must subsequently be conditioned by, and docile to, supranaturally given objective norms. Moreover, the experience to which I want to refer is not simply confined to the conscious sphere, but involves in the first instance the bodily and the sensual.

In speaking of liturgical theology this way, therefore, I am already implying a certain connection to the body and a theology of the body. In a liturgical theology, what is known is precisely what is experienced in the body. Being a communal body of bodies-in-communion, that divine-human reality which is the Church gives rise to a primary theology of the body, a liturgical theology of the body in which the participants are not detached observers, analyzing data external to themselves, but active and passive participants in a drama, bodily recipients of embodied divine acts. From the moment of baptismal initiation, the liturgical experience is a decidedly bodily experience: turned to the east, led to the font, stripped of clothes, immersed in water, anointed with oil, fed with salt, dressed in white. Not all the traditional ritual details need to be preserved for us to notice an explicit body language at work. Here in the liturgy of the Church we discover another primeval "beginning" with its own "original experiences," theologically consonant with, yet symbolically distinct from, the primeval beginning and original experiences contained in the early Genesis narrative and expounded with complex subtlety in the catechetical lectures of John Paul II.

A further task of this book is to outline this liturgical theology of the body with special attention to a dynamic I call "performative nuptiality." This refers to the way in which the liturgy physically *performs* or enacts the spousal union between Christ and his bride. This notion of performativity is of peculiar importance. It expresses the fact that words are often used not simply to express or convey already existing realities, but to bring new states of

6

reality into being. Performativity denotes the sense contained by the Hebrew term *dabar*, which means both word and event. When God speaks, he does not just express his mind or intention. He acts. By speaking, God created a universe out of nothing. By speaking, the prophets shaped history. By speaking, Jesus healed the sick, calmed storms, forgave sins, and raised the dead. Divine action is always word-action, and the divine word is always a performative word, accomplishing what it says.

In the same way, the liturgy of the Church, which is nothing less than the Spirit-filled locus of the incarnate Lord's ongoing redemptive activity in history, must be understood in terms of performative divine action. The divinely-instituted ritual activities of the Church do not indicate or express realities far removed by space or time, nor are they simply commentary on an already current state of affairs. They engage us as performative enactments which actuate and bring to bear the realities they signify in the here and now. Just as John Paul II spoke of a "prophetism of the body" with special reference to the performative character of the marital vows,[9] so we can speak of a "prophetism of the liturgy," in that the drama of the liturgy actually constitutes, as both "announcement" and "cause," the spousal union between Christ and his bride.

To study this performative nuptiality at work, that is, to undertake a liturgical theology of the body as a conscious contribution to John Paul II's invitation to nuptial mysticism, it seems that three prior concepts should be explored. Since a primary or liturgical theology means experiencing, or literally, "suffering" divine activity, it is necessary first to articulate a metaphysics of receptivity in which receptivity finds its proper place in the order of being not simply as indicating a potentiality or lack, but as an activity proper to the being, free development, and perfection of persons. Second, the liturgy itself must be understood in terms of its dramatic character, which involves giving attention not only to ritual action but also to the layout and topology—let us say, the "body language"—of the liturgical space. Third, it seems fitting to specify the relationship between liturgical symbols, the sexed

9 TOB, 534–44.

and sensual human body, and certain transcendent and "semi-tive" signs disclosed through divine revelation.

Having laid out this framework, I will then be in a position to consider three modes in which nuptiality is performed in the divine service: firstly, in the relation between the priest and the people; secondly in the relationship between the proclaimed word and prayer; and thirdly in the relationship between sacrifice and sacrament. Finally, I shall follow this with some concluding remarks on the limitations of performative nuptiality and the liturgical prophetism of the body in light of the great mystery: the eschatological consummation of the marriage between the bride and the Lamb.

1

Passivity and Activity

THE WORD "metaphysics" is usually not welcome in liturgical theology today. Since Martin Heidegger's critique of "onto-theology" (the attempt to fit God and theology into categories belonging to an already worked-out philosophical framework), all talk of being, substance, causality, potency, act and the like is readily dismissed as just another draconian hangover of Aristotelian essentialism. History, culture, and event are now the new defining categories. Liturgical actions are cultural "products" and social "strategies," the gathered community is both interpreter and interpreted, all are engaged in a rich interplay of symbolic personal and political transactions laden with multivalent meanings.

Although such approaches often tend to downplay the reality of the transcendent, and include a bias against objectivity, there is yet much to be learned from them. They put paid to overly mechanical, instrumental, and mathematical modes of theological analysis which reduce the liturgy to a kind of ritualized dispensary for the magical manipulation of reified metaphysical entities. They recall the historical and social embeddedness of ritual meaning, which cannot be extracted and reduced to bare essences independent of the dynamics of body and culture. Above all they alert us to the danger of tying God down and reducing the profoundly symbolic and mysterious character of liturgical action to categories drawn from a single tradition of rational inquiry. Metaphysics is concerned with reason, foundation, definition, intelligibility, *logos*. But the *logos* of the cross, the Christian gospel of a crucified God, cuts through all idolatrous human projects attempting to dominate God, or to calculate and

9

foreordain his rationale. It is along these lines that Louis-Marie Chauvet suggests that true conversion is measured by our movement away from the old metaphysics:

> Can we consent to leave the solid, reassuring ground of our represented foundation and the stable, fixed point in order [to] let ourselves go toward this demanding *letting-be* in which we find ourselves out of our depth?[1]

Having taken all such precautions to heart, however, we must still do metaphysics. That is, we must search for the foundations of what is real. If it is true that the universe has been created and is sustained in being by God through love, then it must be affirmed that there is an intelligibility to the universe, and that love, and all that love implies—relation, mutuality, giving and receiving—is somehow constitutive of what it means to be. This truth opens the way for us to propose a non-idolatrous metaphysics of being, a metaphysics of love. Anterior to every description of a being according to its nature and actions is its intrinsic relation to an active and personal God, its character as fruit of infinite divine generosity, coming from God, existing in God, and destined for God. From this perspective, by knowing what love is, we are afforded insight into what it means *to be* in the deepest sense possible. And because love, in its most perfect form, is interpersonal and relational, one might even say "nuptial,"[2] then personhood and relationality, understood in the context of love, are the keys to the meaning of being.

What might this mean for a liturgical theology of the body? Much in every way, for our understanding of love, personhood and relation can only be mediated bodily: through sense, affectivity, desire. Love is not just a rational choice, the considered fruit of a resolved and steely will. It is born in the heart from the promise of personal encounter, draws into its activity all the

---

1 Louis-Marie Chauvet, *Symbol and Sacrament: A Sacramental Reinterpretation of Christian Existence*, trans. Patrick Madigan and Madeleine Beaumont (Collegeville: Liturgical Press, 1995), 51.

2 In *Deus Caritas Est* (2005) §2, Benedict XVI referred to marital love as "the most perfect image of love" (*amoris per excellentiam imago perfecta*).

impulses and vulnerabilities and energies of body and spirit, and remains ever more deeply open to being affected and changed by the beloved even as it strives for the other's glorious perfection. Purely disinterested love, love that entails no desire or hope for this kind of goal, is characteristic of neither human nor divine love. The inbuilt risk and vulnerability of love, its capacity to wound and displace the self, is not a defect limited to human or creaturely experience; still less is it confined to failed or unrequited love; rather it belongs to love's highest perfection and realization, even—perhaps especially—when that love is God's.

It is from this perspective that I propose the metaphysical foundations that follow. Although I draw on categories and content from the realist Christian metaphysical tradition, I also share Chauvet's concern for the primacy of history, bodily mediation, and "letting-be." I trust that the plausibility and relevance of my synthesis will become clear. For what we can say of the created universe, we can say analogously of the body of Christ, the Church. Just as "the heavens declare the glory of God" (Ps. 19:1), and "the whole earth is full of his glory" (Is. 6:3), so the Church, called into being "for the praise of God's glory" (Eph. 1:12–14), is "the fullness of him who fills all things in every way" (Eph. 1:23). Cosmos and Church are analogously related as arenas of God's glorious deeds and inspired doxology. The ancients, recognizing this connection, understood the unity and good order of the cosmos as intrinsically related to the structure and integrity of divine service. The Church at worship is nothing less than the deified cosmos.[3]

Metaphysics of Receptivity

According to the Christian metaphysical tradition, for a thing to be is for it to be pregnant with activity and meaning.[4] The first act of any real entity is simply existence itself. Before a being is a

3 See Adam G. Cooper, *The Body in St. Maximus the Confessor: Holy Flesh, Wholly Deified* (Oxford: Oxford University Press, 2005), 165–205.

4 In addition to the important work of W. Norris Clarke referenced below I am indebted in this section to certain lines of thought proposed by G.J. McAleer, *Ecstatic Morality and Sexual Politics: A Catholic and Antitotalitarian Theory of*

being of a certain kind, even before we can speak of its nature and potential, it exists![5] What does it mean to say of something, "it exists"? According to Fran O'Rourke, author of one of the most erudite books on the metaphysics of Aquinas, "In reflecting on the mystery of existence, we discern the most profound depth that dwells within each thing, a depth on which all else is grounded."[6] Every finite being irrupts as it were from nothing, not fully-blown and complete to be sure, but real and actual nonetheless. In so doing it simultaneously manifests and conceals in the fact of its "there-ness" a spark of the infinite, absolute existence which is God. In O'Rourke's words: "Existence itself demands that it be infinite, since there is nothing which can limit it. Considered on its own, finite being would seem a contradiction, and is intelligible only in light of the affirmation of infinite creative Being."[7]

From this initial act of existence there issues an innate, purposeful, active flowering towards full development; a dynamic self-communicative impulse in which is manifested "the basic generosity of existence."[8] Like the initial irruption into being, such an act of self-communication implies relation, for by creation there is established a being-in-relation to God: "Being in the sense of existence is nothing other than a being 'towards God.'"[9] Activity meanwhile "places" a thing into a network or world of other beings akin to itself. The emergence from non-being into

---

the Body (New York: Fordham University Press, 2005); David L. Schindler, "The Person: Philosophy, Theology and Receptivity," Communio 21/1 (1994), 172–90; Maurice Nédoncelle, The Personalist Challenge: Intersubjectivity and Ontology, trans. Francois C. Gérard and Francis F. Burch (Eugene, Oregon: Pickwick, 1984); Frederick D. Wilhelmsen, The Metaphysics of Love (London: Sheed and Ward, 1962).

5 Of course I use the word "before" here in the ontological and conceptual sense, not the temporal.

6 Fran O'Rourke, Pseudo-Dionysius and the Metaphysics of Aquinas (Notre Dame: University of Notre Dame Press, 2005), 261.

7 Ibid.

8 Jacques Maritain, Existence and the Existent (Garden City, NY: Doubleday, 1957), 90.

9 Frederick D. Wilhelmsen, The Paradoxical Structure of Existence (Albany, NY: Preserving Christian Publications, 1991), 129.

being is a generation, by loving relation and generous gift, into a mode of shared existence also constituted by loving relation and generous gift. In a word, all being is personal. What we find at the level of human personhood in the form of conscious, volitional and mutual activity is true analogously for all sub-human levels of being as well in their proportionate modes.[10] Nothing created, not even a stone, escapes this law. How much more does it apply in the case of a living being, and above all the living human being, created to image God's essential generosity. Even a being as simple as the two-celled human zygote, who is already a person not simply in potential but in fact, is a being in action and in relation, even if its activity and relation appear, by reason of the primitive stage of development, not yet characteristically personal, remaining open to ever richer actuation.

To be, then, is to be in relation. Not that relation is all there is. The *ad extra* modality of a thing's existence implies its substantial, *ad intra* modality. Relation implies a subject that relates, an "inside," a "starting point."[11] Still, this starting point is itself constituted by relation. Being, activity, and relation are constitutively and mutually proportional. As Josef Pieper puts it, "[t]he higher the form of intrinsic existence, the more developed becomes the relatedness to reality. . . . And the deeper such relations penetrate the world of reality, the more intrinsic becomes the subject's existence."[12]

Human beings, created to manifest and love the triune God, bear in their bodily reality something that reflects God's own character and inner life. What can it be? Our being is composite and contingent, while God's is simple and absolute. Our existence is created and borrowed, while God's is definitively his own. To the extent that our conception of God as perfect being is dominated by the philosophical notion of pure act, the essential characteristic of human existence, receptivity, must always carry with

---

10 See Kenneth L. Schmitz, *The Gift: Creation* (Milwaukee: Marquette University Press, 1982); Eric D. Perl, "'Every Life is a Thought': the Analogy of Personhood in Neoplatonism," *Philosophy and Theology* 18/1 (2006), 143–67.

11 Josef Pieper, *Living the Truth* (San Francisco: Ignatius, 1989), 82.

12 Ibid.

it the notion of imperfection. Receptivity indicates some kind of lack, indeed, a lack of being, and a potency in need of actuation. Here we face an apparent conundrum. On the one hand this receptivity may be taken as the necessary corollary of having been created out of nothing. The human being originates from non-being, and therefore retains this potential for non-being as a constitutive element of his creatureliness. On the other hand, the lack of being indicated by receptivity may be taken as arising from the unrealized potentiality of matter, and therefore forever bound to human physicality. Either way, the innate receptivity that belongs to human nature is associated with lack, not fullness, of being.

Perhaps a step towards the solution of this problem can be had by turning to John Paul II's insights, in his catechetical lectures on marriage and the theology of the body, on the primeval experience of "original solitude" and "the dimension of gift." The lack of being just mentioned seems to be intimated by the divine judgement: it is not good that the man should be alone (Gen. 2:18). At first, all creation is declared "good." Following the creation of man and woman, it is declared "very good." But man alone, the autonomous individual considered in the pure isolation of his undifferentiated generic identity: this is what is "not good."

But what then of receptivity? Is it also "not good"? Not when we realize that to be created means "to have been given being" and "to be a gift." Every human being bears in his or her very physicality the sign of the gift, a sign making visible three things: the one who gives, the identity of the creature as recipient of the gift, and the relation established between giver and receiver. However—and this too is an aspect of original solitude—among all creatures, the human being is uniquely able to perceive and respond to this fact. Constituted in the act of existence by his relation to the divine subject, he too is a subject: *"The structure of his body is such that it permits him to be the author of genuinely human activity."*[13] In the fact of its physicality, the human body reminds the human subject of the essential receptivity that constitutes him as a being, and apart from which he has no being at all.

13 TOB, 154.

Thus for a human to be, according to this anthropological vision, is to be created, to be gifted, and to be a gift. This "basic generosity of existence," to use Maritain's phrase again, is further confirmed not simply by human physicality, but by human sexuality; that is, by the fact that human beings exist as male or female, diverse but complementary ways of being a person in the world. Humanity in general exists as gift in the world, for the world. But human beings in particular exist additionally as gifts for each other. This dimension too belongs to a person's essential receptivity. Only to the degree that a person, as male or female, receives his complementary "other" as a gift, and in turn lives as a gift for his complementary other, is his personhood actualized. But this increasing actualization leads not to greater independence or indifference, but to ever deeper mutuality and receptivity. This is what I mean by associating receptivity with the dimension of the gift:

> In fact, the gift reveals, so to speak, *a particular characteristic of personal existence*, or even of the essence of the person. When God-Yahweh says, "It is not good that the man should be alone" (Gen. 2:18), he affirms that, "alone," the man does not completely realize this essence. He realizes it only by existing *"with someone"*—and, put even more deeply and completely, by existing *"for someone."*[14]

But is receptivity only a condition of *material* existence? God, whose "image" is reflected in the essential receptivity proper to physical and sexed human existence, is not material, but pure spirit. Human physicality alone does not express the divine image, or if it does, then all non-human bodies, by virtue of their physicality, also bear the same image. To be sure, some divine trace (*vestigium*), some dynamic stamp of eternal wisdom, is present in every finite creature: all things really participate in and therefore reflect the fecund generosity of the self-diffusive divine goodness. But what is it that makes the image borne by human beings unique? And how can this image be characterized by receptivity, if God is pure act?

14 Ibid., 182.

One way of answering this question would be to recognize the kind of relationship that exists between image and impress. Nowhere do the Scriptures identify human beings as an "image" of God, simply. The Fathers of the Church, attentive to the nuances of the biblical text, commonly remarked how human beings are said to have been created "according to" the image of God; Christ alone is that image proper (Col. 1:15).[15] For the Greek mind, the metaphor invoked by comparison of an image proper to that which is according to the image is that of an original and a copy. On the one hand there is the positive original seal or stamp of some sort, and on the other hand there is the negative impression left by it in wax or clay.

Using this metaphor to help explore the conceptual question at hand, we can explain the (negative) receptivity of the being created according to the image of God with reference to the (positive) active agency of the original. On this score, the essential receptivity of human personhood is simply the reverse side, the passive consequence, of the essential activity of the God who created it.

But there is another way of answering the question of whether there might be something in God's own inner life to which the essential receptivity of human personhood bears witness. Traditional Christian interpretation of the life and person of Christ, the definitive visible image of the invisible God, has always acknowledged the essential reciprocity between Jesus, the Son who comes from Father, and God the Father who sent him. Jesus appears in history as the Son who is loved by the Father and known by the Father. The Son obeys the Father, does his work, and receives his authority and glory. This Son of God, active co-divine agent of creation and redemption, who has been and is always "one" with the Father (Jn. 10:30), stands in an essentially receptive relation to the Father, not only in the actions of the economy, but eternally, in the mysterious intimacy of trinitarian knowledge and love: "No one has ever seen God, but the only-

15 In his earlier works Augustine equated the "image of God" of Genesis 1:26 with Christ the Son. Later he identifies every human being as a living *imago Trinitatis*.

begotten, who is in the Father's bosom, has made him known" (Jn. 1:18). Or to put it in more philosophical terms,

> [T]he Father, unoriginated possessor of the infinite fullness of the divine nature, communicates ecstatically his entire divine nature to the Second Person, the Son or Word, in an act of loving self-knowledge, so that the only distinction between them is the distinction of two complementary but opposed relations, Giver and Receiver. . . . Thus the very inner life of God himself, the supreme fullness of what it means to be, is by its very nature *self-communicative Love*, which then subsequently flows over freely into the finite self-communication that is creation.[16]

If this is how God is, if reciprocity and therefore receptivity are proper to his inner life as Father in relation to the Son, then those beings who bear his image, who issue into existence in time from the eternally creative and fecund fount of that relation, must also carry in themselves an essential receptivity that indicates not so much some lack of being as the very clue to understanding the way to human perfection. Just as in the Trinity there is a certain kind of active passivity, a receptive "letting be" by which the Son is freely begotten and the Spirit freely proceeds from the eternal giving of the Father,[17] so it is as a person receives, is acted upon, and gives that he most perfectly "is." This is not to deny that being is perfected in act. It is rather to say that receptivity is ineradicably inscribed within act. It is to specify the nature of activity in terms of a free and conscious receptivity, a receptivity to divine love.

It is not improper to conceive of God by way of analogy as pure act, in which there lies no unrealized potential whatsoever. But if this is true, then relation, a crucial constituent of being, must likewise be perfectly actualized in God. It cannot be acci-

---

16 W. Norris Clarke, *Person and Being* (Milwaukee: Marquette University Press, 1993), 12.

17 See Hans Urs von Balthasar, *Theo-Drama: Theological Dramatic Theory*, vol. 5: *The Last Act*, trans. Graham Harrison (San Francisco: Ignatius, 1998), 85–91.

dental but must be constitutive to God's being. This proposal is confirmed and illuminated in Christian revelation in the mystery of the holy Trinity: God is innately a triadic, eternal unity of self-communicating, generously self-diffusive being, knowledge and love. To be is to be in act, and to be in act is to be receptively in mutual relation. Or put another way, the *imago dei* in man is an *imago trinitatis*. Here, in outline, is a metaphysic of receptivity.

Eros and Ecstasis

Much of what I have been trying to say in the foregoing section is summed up in this statement of the metaphysical vision of Aquinas: "Divine love is the principle of the universe in its origin, its internal order and immanent dynamism, and its ultimate finality."[18]

The name given to this principle early in the Greek philosophical tradition was *eros*. *Eros* is the dynamic built into the cosmos in its continual movement from potentiality to actuality. Matter yearns for form; the potential yearns for actualization; all things yearn for their good. Eros is this fundamental disposition of all things to move towards their proper good and perfection. It is the universal, innate purposefulness in things.

This restless desire for perfection present in all beings manifests itself in the human person as an appetite for completion, for an ultimate happy end. This is a goal we cannot *not* want. Of itself, *eros* proffers no help in determining the relative quality of the particular objects that pose themselves as ends worthy of pursuit. Strictly speaking, it does not belong to raw desire to judge. That is because, precisely in so far as it is a human *passion*, *eros* is not so much something a person does, as something he suffers. This is not to say that a person has no control over his or her desires, nor that desire, appropriately trained and formed, does not play a vital role in making sound moral judgements. Indeed, Aristotle defined the passions as *enhyloi logoi*, physically instantiated rational impulses, while John Paul II believed that the physical and affective drives are rightly thought to bear real "rational

18 O'Rourke, *Pseudo-Dionysius and the Metaphysics of Aquinas*, 225.

indications."[19] It does mean, however, that desire or *eros* or passion is, by definition, a reaction before it is an action. *Eros* "happens" when something external to us, coming within the purview of our perception, attracts us, arouses our response, and moves us to want it. The action of *eros* begins outside of us; only secondarily may we be said to be its subjects. We suffer the activity of something good, and only then recognize its goodness. As Paul Wadell writes:

> Appetites respond, they reach out only because they have first felt the touch of another thing's goodness. Consider how we know something to be good. We do not declare its value, we feel its value. Hearing a Mozart symphony, it is not so much we who say it is beautiful, but the music which says it to us. . . . If we desire anything, it is only because we have first experienced its goodness.[20]

Notice here the place of beauty in its relation to desire. Beauty, as the splendid radiance of truth, is naturally attractive and worthy of desire. As a human passion, *eros* places us in purposive relation to the good, the true, and the beautiful, so that we reach out to that which has first taken hold of us. The erotic experience of beauty implies a real, inner reception of the form of the good. Aquinas speaks of "a sense of affinity" with the beautiful or good. It leaves its "imprint" in us. It is this real change in the sufferer of beauty or goodness which is called love. By it "the lover stands in relation to that which he loves, as though it were himself or part of himself."[21]

Every created being acts from its desires. This also applies to human beings. Even though characteristically human action is set apart from instinctive and sub-human activity by its volitional and purposeful quality, the motivating dynamic for much human action stems in part from impulses that lie beneath the level of the conscious. Every person acts as he does with certain goals,

---

19 John Paul II, *Veritatis Splendor* (1993) §48.

20 Paul Wadell, *The Primacy of Love: An Introduction to the Ethics of Thomas Aquinas* (New York / Mahwah: Paulist Press, 1992), 82.

21 Thomas Aquinas, *Summa Theologiae* [hereafter = ST] I–II, 26, 2.

ends and purposes in view. These purposes are shaped and determined by that person's multi-level range of desires, dispositions, loves, needs, and wants. And since we become what we do, a person is shaped by, or even *is*, his or her appetites.

But the human person is not just a material being, bound to physical and biological laws. Our desires arise not only from the material and organic level, but from the sensual, affective, cognitive, and spiritual levels as well. The human person is an integral spiritual being, and thus, within certain limits, is free and able to determine his desires himself. As *dominus sui*, a self-possessed master of himself, the human person is able, on the basis of higher-order desires, to direct his lower-order desires this way or that, to fashion them, within the concrete conditions of his life, into a project. True, any conflicting desires and intentions will also manifest themselves, one way or another, in his acts. But as he matures, he can increasingly come to recognize and master such intentions, suitably unifying, integrating and directing them towards certain goods more or less intelligently selected, ordered, and pursued. This does not mean that desire gives way to insensible rationality. The mature human life, the perfect life, is in its entirety "a holy longing."[22]

Since love is a reaching-out, a longing for union with the object of desire, it further belongs to *eros* to lead to *ecstasis*, a going out of oneself towards the beloved. Not only is all creation instilled with a "divine yearning" (*theios eros*), but God himself can in some sense be regarded as an "erotic" being. His love is not only creative of the good in a detached, disinterested way. Rather, his love draws him out of himself, ecstatically, into its objects. Moreover, his relation with creation is such that he desires its response. To be sure, God loves freely, unconditionally, with no strings attached. His self-diffusive goodness constitutes the being and goodness of all that is. Yet his love for the world does not leave him unmoved, but reaches its peak, as it were, in the incarnation, in which God actually becomes the object of his desire.

Origen of Alexandria was among the first to defend the applicability of the term *eros* to the kind of divine love the Bible refers

---

22 Dionysius the Areopagite, *Divine Names* 4, 10.

to as *agape*.[23] Consider this passage from his great *Commentary on the Song of Songs*, where "the soul" and the spousal Church are reciprocally analogous:

> Indeed, the soul is led by a heavenly love and desire, and, once the beauty and glory of the Word of God has been perceived, it falls in love with his splendour and by this receives from him some dart and wound of love.... And it will receive from him the saving wound and will burn with the blessed fire of his holy love.[24]

Similarly, according to the Dionysian mystical vision, later affirmed by Thomas Aquinas, the whole universe is a revelation of divine *eros*, inasmuch as God is the cause of all good, whose longing for good issues forth in the creation of all things: "That yearning which creates all the goodness of the world pre-existed superabundantly within the Good and did not allow it to remain without issue. It stirred him to use the abundance of his powers in the production of the world."[25] This ecstatic procession of the divine good in creation reaches its climax in the Incarnation, in which God, out of love for humankind, actually became the object of his love. Here, without in any way diminishing his own being, the divine lover leaves himself, passing into the object of his love in such a way that his goodness "leaves its imprint" con-

---

23 This association was famously challenged in the 1930s by the Lutheran theologian Anders Nygren in *Agape and Eros*, trans. Philip S. Watson (London: SPCK, 1953). For discussion of how Nygren's position overlooks key biblical data, as well as ends up negating the creaturely integrity of the human being, see Ceslaus Spicq, *Agape in the New Testament* 3 vols. (St. Louis and London: Herder, 1966); D.C. Schindler, "The Redemption of Eros: Philosophical Reflections on Benedict XVI's First Encyclical," *Communio* 33 (2006), 375–99; Josef Pieper, *Faith, Hope, Love* (San Francisco: Ignatius, 1997); Ysabel D'Andia, "Eros and Agape: The Divine Passion of Love," *Communio* 24 (1997), 29–50; Henri de Lubac, "Eros and Agape," in id., *Theological Fragments* (San Francisco: Ignatius, 1989); Catherine Osborne, *Eros Unveiled: Plato and the God of Love* (Oxford: Clarendon Press, 1994).

24 Origen, in the prologue to his *Commentary on the Song of Songs*, in *Origen: An Exhortation to Martyrdom, et al*, trans. Rowan A. Greer (London: SPCK, 1979), 223.

25 Dionysius the Areopagite, *Divine Names* 4, 10. Cf. ST I, 20, 2.

cretely in history, arousing a real change and "sense of affinity" on the part of those who encounter and suffer its beauty. We are drawn to love God from the love revealed and concretely enacted in the person of Christ, coming into relation with him as though he were ourselves or a part of ourselves. And indeed, there is no "as though" to it: in Christ, God loves humanity in a connatural union, making our flesh and blood humanity his very own (Heb. 2:10–14). Speaking of his beloved friends, Christ can say, in Augustine's paraphrase, "In me they too are I myself."[26] *Eros* does not necessarily indicate a lack on the part of its subject. Indeed, it is precisely out of the pregnant fullness of his own trinitarian self-love that God has gone out of himself and become the object of his love, so that we in turn, filled with his love, may go out of ourselves and become divine. Having suffered the ecstatic love of God, we are moved to become subjects of ecstatic love for God. Dionysius finds the example of ecstatic *eros* in St. Paul especially striking:

> This is why the great Paul, swept along by his yearning for God and seized of its ecstatic power, had this inspired word to say: "It is no longer I who live, but Christ who lives in me." Paul was truly a lover and, as he says, he was beside himself for God, possessing not his own life but the life of the One for whom he yearned, as exceptionally beloved.[27]

We are our desires. We become what we love. If what we love is other than ourself, then love involves us in a real ecstasis, a going out of ourselves and becoming another. Far from diminishing our being, ecstatic love, when directed towards God who alone is truly good, accomplishes the fulfilment of our being. That is why, says Aquinas, "it is better to love God than to know him."[28] Moreover, there lies an inner affinity between the deep dynamisms of erotic enchantment and the single-minded resolve embodied in a completely outgoing, oblative love. As Angelo Scola asserts:

26 Augustine, *Tractates on the Gospel of John* 108, 5.
27 Dionysius the Areopagite, *Divine Names* 4, 2.
28 *Melior est amor Dei quam cognitio.* ST I, 82, 3.

It is right to say that every act of love, even the most radically disinterested, implies a certain "taking pleasure" (*complacentia*) of the subject in his own good.... [T]his love cannot be defined as egotistical because it is exercised before the question of interest or disinterest comes into play. It is an original "taking pleasure" which the subject cannot *not* encounter on the path toward his realization. . . .[29]

Thus even the most radical acts of discipleship and self-renunciation for the sake of the kingdom "are born from this 'desiring' structure of the 'I.'"[30] If human beings have been created for communion with God, if the final development of our purposive dispositions consists in union with him, then we become more really ourselves, not less, by loving him. All depends on our suffering his love, on receiving his goodness and beauty, so that he alone becomes our ultimate object of desire.

Suffering Divine Things

So far in this chapter I have said very little about "nuptiality." I have sought rather to provide a kind of background metaphysical and anthropological framework by which to make sense of what goes on in the Church's worship insofar as it is a performative, divine-human nuptial act. In both Israelite and Christian worship, there has always been a sense that what takes place in the words and rites of the liturgy is, as it were, an active "letting be" for God to enter into an erotic, nuptial bond of union with his bride, the new Jerusalem, so that it can be said: "Now the dwelling of God is with men, and he will live with them" (Rev. 21:3). While the liturgy certainly requires certain human acts to be performed and certain human words to be spoken, the primary word-acts are God's. It is his humanward movement that stirs and awakens love, his philanthropic ecstasis that in the liturgy "leaves its imprint" on the individual and collective heart, enabling the body to breathe.

29 Angelo Scola, *The Nuptial Mystery,* trans. Michelle K. Borras (Grand Rapids: Eerdmans, 2005), 71.
30 Ibid.

In every celebration of the liturgy therefore the hypostatic union is somehow made present and consummated anew. Put another way, only in Christian worship are the conditions for human life and perfection fulfilled. The liturgy constitutes the symbolic and historically concrete medium in which the reciprocal phases of the divine-human marriage find enactment: activity and passivity, reception and gift. The liturgy reinforces the truth that human beings do not contain within themselves the active principle of their own fulfilment and perfection. The highest goods always come to us in the manner of a divine gift.[31] In the liturgy we give ourselves in faith, hope and love over to the promise of this gratuitous exchange. As Aquinas and other great teachers have always insisted, "only God deifies."[32]

Maximus the Confessor made the same point when he discussed the interplay between activity and passivity in the unfolding of the human vocation. Since deification consists in the final entry into the promised state of rest, it requires the cessation of all natural activity and total surrender to the infinite, supernatural action of God. Passivity, not activity, provides the raw material for God to assimilate human nature to his own infinite beauty:

> For nothing created is by nature capable of deification. . . .
> For it is intrinsic and peculiar to divine grace alone to bestow deification proportionately on beings, for only divine grace illuminates nature with supernatural light and elevates nature beyond its proper limits in excess of glory.[33]

Clearly the kind of "passivity" implied here has nothing to do with passionless indifference. On the contrary, suffering divine things represents the pinnacle of human development, not as the fruit of our native potential, but the Spirit-led integration and concentration of all the dynamic energies of our organic, affective, and spiritual drives into a focused, single-hearted willingness

---

31 See the masterful development of this fundamental anthropological truth by Josef Pieper, *Divine Madness: Plato's Case against Secular Humanism*, trans. Lothar Krauth (San Francisco: Ignatius, 1995), 7, 16–17, 37–58.

32 *Solus Deus deificat.* ST I–II, 112, 1.

33 Maximus the Confessor, *Responses to Thalassius* 22.

to be captivated by divine love. Nor does this happen automatically, by simple exposure to the liturgical events. To be sure, the sacraments are effective *ex opere operato*, but the mature, love-formed faith which they alone make possible only arises as the fruit of a moral and spiritual project, a co-operative venture in which God, taking the initiative, woos the soul into learning his ways, suffering his grace, freely permitting its interior actualisation to come from without.

We may illumine this claim by mentioning John Paul II's insistence on the vital mutual relation between the "ethical" and "erotic." The discovery of the true meaning of bodily life, which involves the experience of erotic love,

> is the task of the human spirit, and it is by its nature an ethical task. If one does not assume this task, the very attraction of the senses and the passion of the body can stop at mere concupiscence, deprived of all ethical value.[34]

Applying this insight to a liturgical theology of the body would suggest that assimilation to God in the liturgy is not a matter of pure aesthetic or emotional experience, still less of mechanical cause and effect, but of voluntary integration of the sensory passions to the "noble pleasure"[35] of love for God, in response to divine action. Intensity of passion *per se* should not therefore be taken as a sure sign of divine-human nuptiality, that is, as a sure sign of the spiritual efficacy of liturgical acts. As Plato's Socrates warns, "Not every love, but only that which has a noble purpose, is noble and worthy of praise."[36] An act of judgement, the clear-eyed vision of rightly formed faith, is needed. The passion of eros must be guided by truth, so that what we consent to suffer is really the effective love of God in Christ, in other words, that which is really and ultimately good and beautiful, and not simply that which falsely presents itself to our blind and eager yearnings as such. At least this is what must take place if we are to worship the Father "in spirit and in truth" (Jn. 4:23–24).

34 TOB, 319.
35 Ibid., 320.
36 *Symposium* 181.

2

Drama and Ritual

HISTORY IS SOMETIMES likened to a stage on which the countless members of the human race act out their lives in a vast, interconnected drama. Shakespeare's immortal lines express this idea in a tragic, even fatalistic vein:

> All the world's a stage,
> And all the men and women merely players. . . .[1]

The divine liturgy can also be likened to a stage on which the Church acts in her members. But in this case the image is much more positive and hopeful, for through the liturgy the Church unfolds all the riches of her innermost being, publicly enacting her saving story within the horizon of human and cosmic history. At one level, the liturgy may be thought of simply as that complex of external, ordered, and structural forms in and by which the Church worships God. But as an outward, visible structure, the liturgy forms an essential dimension of the Church's inward, "spiritual" worship. Precisely because it is the means of worship, the liturgy becomes the concrete way in which the Church constitutes herself *qua* the Church, that is, as the body of Christ. For the Church is by nature a cultic community. To be the Church is to worship. As Orthodox theologian Alexander Schmemann put it, worship is

> the public act which externally actualizes the nature of the Church as the Body of Christ, an act, moreover, that is not partial . . . but which embraces, expresses, inspires and

---

1 William Shakespeare, *As You Like It* Act II, Scene 7.

27

defines the whole Church, her whole essential nature, her whole life.[2]

This worship, moreover, is essentially eucharistic (Rev. 11:16–17). It is defined by the two-dimensional action of the risen Lord who, associating the assembled members of his body with himself, offers up thanks to the Father, and pours out on them his redeeming and sanctifying Spirit.

In worship, then, the Church acts according to her nature. In praying, she is "entirely what she ought to be. . . ."[3] In particular it is in her eucharist, her faith-filled sacrifice of thanksgiving, that she comes to "subsist," that is, that she becomes a concrete, spatially embodied, unified subject. By it she fulfils her divine vocation to exist "for the praise of God's glory." By it she constitutes herself as "the fullness of him who fills all things in every way," "the dwelling in which God lives by his Spirit," the christoform body in which the universe glimpses "the multifaceted wisdom of God" (Eph. 1:12, 23; 2:22; 3:10).

These few phrases, drawn from the splendid letter to the Ephesians, make it clear that even as the Church becomes a subject, even as she acts as herself, the primary actor in the unfolding drama of her liturgy is Christ. It is Christ who calls the Church together into an assembly of faith. It is Christ who addresses her with words of forgiveness and life. It is Christ who cleanses, feeds, and nourishes her as "flesh of his flesh, bone of his bones." This is not just a pious idea, but actual and tangible. As David Bird writes:

> By the power of the Spirit, Christ speaks through the readings, presides through the priest, exhorts through the sermon, and sings and prays through the hymns and prayers of the community, illuminating the minds of those taking part in accordance with their faith.[4]

---

2 Alexander Schmemann, *Introduction to Liturgical Theology,* trans. Ashleigh E. Moorhouse (New York: St. Vladimir's Seminary Press, 1996), 14.

3 Hans Urs von Balthasar, *Explorations in Theology II: The Spouse of the Word,* trans. A. V. Littledale (San Francisco: Ignatius, 1991), 461.

4 David Bird, *Heaven Revealed: The Holy Spirit and the Mass* (Leominster, Herefordshire: Gracewing, 2008), 11.

Christ is not just a memory in the minds of the worshipping faithful, but the present high priest, the leading liturgist, who, according to the writer to the Hebrews, speaks and embodies the divine name in person and grants access to the mercy of the Father precisely in the midst of his assembled brothers and sisters (Heb. 2:11–13; 4:14–16).

In this way we see that the Church is and remains herself only as Christ acts in her, for her, through her. This is not to rob her of her proper activity. It is rather a fact in keeping with a metaphysic of receptivity and erotic ecstasis, according to which the Church's constitutive activity as a subsistent subject consists foremost in receiving life from God, in accepting her existence as pure gift, in letting Christ be her head and self, in suffering the redeeming action of his love. What John Paul II says of spouses and their bodies can also be said of Christ and his ecclesial body: "Through love, the wife's 'I' becomes, so to speak, the husband's 'I.' The body is the expression of this 'I,' it is the basis of its identity."[5] As Karl Adam once put it, "Christ the Lord is the real self of the Church."[6] Here is the essence of the Johannine "I in them and you in me" (Jn. 17:23). The eucharistic worship which constitutes the essence of the Church's identity, the act by which she can say "I" as a subject, which amounts to Christ saying "I" through her, is the action that most adequately corresponds to her living experience of paternal, divine love. Her *eu-charist* only arises from her experience of *charis*.

Liturgy as Theodrama

On the basis of these introductory remarks I would like in this chapter to unfold the significance of the Church's liturgy as a ritualized divine drama, or to use von Balthasar's celebrated term, a "theodrama." There are hints in the New Testament that this "dramatic" way of conceiving the Church's worship was already entertained in the apostolic era. Consider for example St. Paul's

---

5 TOB, 611.

6 Karl Adam, *The Spirit of Catholicism*, trans. Dom Justin McCann (London: Sheed and Ward, 1929), 15.

curious use of the Greek word *prographein* in Galatians 3:1. To people who had almost certainly never witnessed the events of Calvary in person the Apostle declares: "Before your very eyes Christ was clearly portrayed [*proegraphē*] as crucified." Where, when, and in what form did this manifestly visible "portrayal" take place? If Paul had in mind only some prior verbal or written presentation of the narrative contents of the Church's primitive *kerygma*, why does he employ this emphatic "before your very eyes" (*kat' ophthalmous*)?

This is not to suggest that Paul is referring here to some kind of re-enactment of the crucifixion along the lines of a modern passion play. His remark does seem to carry more than purely rhetorical force, however.[7] Is it not possible that it suggests rather, in Paul's understanding, that the saving works of God in Christ have been more than simply preached in his readers' hearing, but dramatically, visibly, and efficaciously *enacted* among them? Could not the Apostle's personal characterization of his ministry as liturgical and priestly (Rom. 15:16) be more than metaphorical?

A second example illustrating the theodramatic self-understanding of the early Church's public liturgy can be found in the appearance narrative in Luke 24:36–53, a pericope apparently structured according to the form of a liturgical ritual, with the risen Lord Jesus as the main actor. Its main components include Christ's bestowal of peace on the gathered disciples (24:36), his self-revelation by means of the eucharistic meal (24:37–43), his explanation of the Old Testament Scriptures with reference to their fulfilment in his saving death and resurrection (24:44–49), and his bestowal of the priestly blessing (24:50–53). If it is true that this structure partially derives from and reflects the concrete liturgical practice of the early Christians, then it seems plausible

---

7 Some commentators put Paul's choice of words here down to "a case of self-ironic exaggeration." See Hans Dieter Betz, *Galatians: A Commentary on Paul's Letter to the Churches in Galatia* (Philadelphia: Fortress Press, 1979), 131; cf. the more nuanced position of Schrenk, "*prographo*," in Gerhard Kittel, ed. *Theological Dictionary of the New Testament*. vol. I (Grand Rapids: Eerdmans, 1964), 770–1.

to suggest that they construed their liturgy as a dramatic, ritually embodied encounter with the risen Lord.

Examples can be multiplied when we turn to the post-apostolic period and the Fathers of the Church. Here we find increasingly explicit references to the dramatic presence and action of Christ in the liturgical assembly. The events of salvation history in Israel and Christ are so many theodramatic *mysteria* whose supernatural, salvific efficacy flows beyond the limits of their natural, historically specific situation.[8] As "the place of sacrifice," the worshipping Church constitutes the living space in which these *mysteria* are effectually re-actualized. The bishops who teach divine realities and who preside over the assembly's ordered dramatic acts are living embodiments of Christ and the Father.[9] What has been said with reference to the mystagogy of Maximus the Confessor is equally applicable to the whole patristic worldview: "the liturgy is everywhere presupposed as the act that makes real the universal presence of the hypostatic Christ."[10] In sum, participation in the liturgy spells participation in the dramatic, redemptive deeds of God, whose culminating point lies in the paschal mystery.

Ritual Performativity

The notion of performativity in speech and language was famously elaborated by philosopher John L. Austin in his 1962 book, *How to Do Things with Words*. Paying close attention to the actual ways we use language, Austin noticed that we commonly use words not simply to describe an already existing state of affairs, but to bring a new one into being. Performative or "constative" speech, in distinction from indicative or descriptive speech, refers to speech used to perform an action, words spoken so as to effect a new reality. Examples include the naming of a

8 This is brought out clearly by Jean Daniélou, *The Bible and the Liturgy* (London: Darton, Longman and Todd, 1960).

9 Ignatius, *Eph.* 5.2; *Trall.* 7.2; *Phil.* 4; *Magn.* 3.1; 6.1.

10 Hans Urs von Balthasar, *Cosmic Liturgy: The Universe According to Maximus the Confessor*, trans. Brian E. Daley (San Francisco: Ignatius, 2003), 316.

ship, "I name this ship. . . ," uttered when launching it with a bottle; the contracting of a marriage, "I take you. . . ," uttered during the marriage ceremony; or the making of a bet, "I bet you five dollars. . . ," and so on. These examples bring to our notice that often the important thing in speech is not only what the words say, but what the words do. Attending to the performative dimension of language requires attending to the dynamic context in which certain words are uttered.

Of course, this idea of performativity in language is by no means new to theology. The Scriptures often tie formal speech-acts to the effectuation of a new reality. We need only think of the *lux fiat* of creation (Gen. 1:3), the bestowal of blessing in the priestly liturgy (Num. 6:23), not to mention the numerous speech-acts of Christ by which he stilled the storm, healed the sick, forgave sins, raised the dead, and bestowed his Spirit, all of which demonstrate the effective dynamism of divine speech: "He spoke, and it came to be" (Ps. 33:9). It is just because Christ is God that his words effect what they signify. More than that, he is the Word of God in person, the personal embodiment of creative divine speech, by whom all things came into and are kept in being (Col. 1:16; Heb. 1:3). Christ is God's speech-act made flesh.

Moreover, this Spirit-empowered performativity of the divine word by no means ceased with the earthly ministry of Jesus. The effective operation of his word continues in the liturgical ministry of his appointed heralds. St. Paul ascribes the efficacy of his preaching to the powerful activity of the Spirit (1 Cor. 2:4). The word of God, proclaimed by the Apostles, is a deadly sword, an effective spiritual weapon and diagnostic tool (Eph. 6:17; Heb. 4:12; Rev. 1:16). Above all, it is the dynamic force that elicits human faith (Rom. 10:17), so that even the sacraments, sometimes referred to as "visible words," ultimately derive their causative power from the divine word. It is the word which attaches to the element that makes it a sacrament.[11] Aquinas, with this famous formula of Augustine in mind, repeatedly refers the effective power of the Church's sacraments to their original divine institution. "The sacraments attain their effect through the force

11 Augustine, *Tractates on the Gospel of John* 80, 3.

of their institution."[12] As instrumental causes of divine grace, "they effect what they signify" not by their natural symbolic power but on account of their divinely imbued salvific energy. Luther's objection to the penitential system operative in his day arose in large part from his belief that it had lost sight of just this performative dynamic. To his mind, the efficacy of the sacrament of penance had come to rest almost entirely on subjective and psychological factors instead of in the objective, performative speech-act of the priest in the person of Christ. What was needed was a return to faith in the *verbum efficax*, the authoritative, faith-creating promise of God, physically embodied and orally enacted in the dominically instituted sacramental ministry of the Church.[13] Luther would have endorsed Pope Benedict XVI's assertion that the Christian gospel does not just impart information, but is a performative communication that "makes things happen and is life-changing."[14]

I said above that through her eucharist in particular the Church is effectively constituted as the Church, a subject whose "I" is Christ himself. The eucharistic liturgy constitutes a dramatically enacted nuptial performance whose efficacy rests on the grace causing, deifying power of the divine word. A close analogy is found in the sacramental rite of marriage with its performative formula of consent: "I take you to be my wife / my husband." In the performance of this unique speech-act, two persons, a man and a woman, effectively become a single subject, "the actual subject of the married vocation and life."[15] Yet we know that these words do not yet consummate marriage in its fullness. The words must become flesh; there must be a passage from the marriage vows to conjugal intercourse, which is *"the reality* that corresponds to these words."[16] But this correspondence is not incidental to the realization of the reality. The vows

---

12 ST III, 38, 3; also ST III, 62, 1; III, 60, 5.

13 I discuss this emphasis further in *Life in the Flesh: An Anti-Gnostic Spiritual Philosophy* (Oxford: Oxford University Press, 2008), 108–30.

14 Benedict XVI, *Spe Salvi* (2007) §2–3.

15 TOB, 531.

16 TOB, 532.

stipulate "a clearly determined content," a content that in its turn corresponds with the form of the covenant instituted by God at "the beginning" and realized in Christ's cruciform self-sacrifice. The free, exclusive, total, mutual, and permanent self-donation performatively enacted in the vows has a prophetic character in as much as "it is *the proclamation of the truth that comes from God* and in some sense the act of stating this truth in the name of God. . . ."[17] All the fundamental meanings of the body and marriage, including its procreative meaning, "are initiated and in a certain sense 'programmed' in a comprehensive way in conjugal consent."[18] The marriage rite is simultaneously a performative and prophetic nuptial enactment, referring backwards to its institution by God, and forward to its physical consummation in the truth.

In a similar way, the eucharistic liturgy of the Church embodies both these performative and prophetic dimensions, referring backwards to salvation history and its culmination in the *pascha* of Christ, and forward—with a sense of incompleteness and yearning—to the eschatological consummation at the resurrection. This two-way reference by no means detracts from the eucharist's intrinsic, effectual power to achieve hiddenly here and now all that it signifies. The ritual words of the eucharistic liturgy do not express mere intentions and wishes on the part of its speakers, nor simply describe what is already the case. With reference to the words of institution, Romano Guardini states:

> He [Christ] does not say: "Pray God to do thus," but simply "do." Thus he places in human hands an act which can be fulfilled only by the divine. . . . Man acts; but in his human action is the act of God. And not only in the general sense that God is present in all human endeavor because all our reality and strength, wisdom and will come from Him. This is a specific, historical act; here the word *institution* has a special, unique significance. God determined, proclaimed, and

17 TOB, 540.
18 Ibid., 543.

instituted; man is to execute the act. When he does so, God makes of it something of which he alone is capable.[19]

In fact the performative words of the eucharistic liturgy do more than simply effect a change in the sacramental species. By consenting in faith to Christ's covenantal proposal, by saying "yes" to his self-donation by means of this performative *anamnesis* of his death, the Church, like Mary, "gives body" to Christ. Colman O'Neill explains:

> [The Church's] sacramental ceremonies give Christ a new bodily form on earth; not a new body, for he has only one; but an extension to his body, or better, a transposition of his body into a new dimension. The ritual actions which constitute the essential parts of the sacramental ceremonial and the materials employed in these actions provide the means by which the risen Christ is bodily present and bodily active in the Church. The economy of incarnation is here brought a stage further than in Palestine. *External expressions of faith* in the incarnation become themselves the material of incarnation.[20]

Ritual Topography

From early in pre-Christian Jewish thought the layout, furnishings, orientation, and ritual actions of the Temple or place of worship were held to be of determinative significance. Philo of Alexandria, a contemporary of the Apostle Paul, gave voice to a long tradition in Jewish liturgical exegesis when he designated the Temple in Jerusalem, built according to a divinely revealed blueprint, as representative of the entire cosmos, a paradise in miniature, with the high priest as the mediator between earth and heaven and the twice-daily sacrificial liturgy an act of thanksgiving by God's people on behalf of the whole human race, a

---

19 Romano Guardini, *Preparing Yourself for Mass* (Manchester, NH: Sophia Institute Press, 1993), 71.

20 Colman E. O'Neill, *Meeting Christ in the Sacraments* (NY: Alba House, 1991, rev. ed.), 37.

public service whose performance ensured the stability of the created order.[21] The fact that in the Bible the Hebrew *maqôm* and Greek *topos* came to be used as another way of designating the Temple or cultic locus highlights the importance of the spatial and dramatic for Christian worship.[22] In this attachment of symbolic value to features of ritual topography we may discern a kind of liturgical metaphysics according to which the Church's liturgy constitutes a progressive series of unfolding symbolic, theandric activities through which the hidden, eschatological union of the cosmos in and with God is manifested and realized in historic time.

If we call this interpretation of the liturgy iconographic or architectonic, we see how opposed it is to all functional and utilitarian interpretations of the church building and the liturgy. According to iconographic interpretation such matters as architecture, orientation, and ritual movement are by no means incidental to faithful liturgical enactment. The church building and the liturgy enacted therein have an appropriate body language: they are patterned on and meant effectually to embody true and transcendent realities. Not only the liturgy, but also the building conveys certain meanings and ideas, and with this expression is implied the possibility of falsification. Of every church building one is obliged to ask: what does it say? There can be no doubt that it speaks. "If the [true] meanings are not made manifest in the architecture, then the symbolic means of architecture will be 'speaking' of something different."[23]

The meaning or rationale of the language we are elaborating finds primary expression not firstly in exterior physical features, but interiorly, in the altar: "For it is in their interpretations of the altar," interpretations physically and spatially embodied in the

---

21 See C.T.R. Hayward, *The Jewish Temple: A Non-biblical Sourcebook* (London: Routledge, 1996).

22 See Gen. 22:4; 28:17; Ex. 24:9–11; Dt. 12:5–9; Jn. 11:48; 1 Clem. 5.4–7.

23 R. Maguire and K. Murray, *Modern Churches of the World* (London: Studio Vista, 1965), 9; quoted by Steven J. Schloeder, *Architecture in Communion: Implementing the Second Vatican Council through Liturgy and Architecture* (San Francisco: Ignatius, 1998), 173.

concrete details of liturgical topography and ritual drama, "that adherents of the various Christian confessions reveal their real and fundamental differences. . . ."[24] The altar in all religions is the place of sacrifice, the medium of man's offering and holocaust to the gods. In biblical religion, however, the altar is first the dwelling place of God's glory, the place at which Yahweh meets with his people in mercy, the place at which his goodness is visibly and audibly revealed (2 Chr. 7:1–3): "It was the ritual bridge between heaven and earth, the point of contact between the Lord and his people."[25] It is because the altar is the medium of God's service to man that it is able to become the medium of man's service to God. Pieper cites the old rule that the altar be made of stone, not wood, "in accordance with its significative meaning," which lies in the fact that the rock is Christ, "the archetypal sacrificial victim," whose altar is the cross.[26] Schloeder asserts the centrality of the altar for the entire church building; as the sign of Christ himself, it is the building's *raison d'être*.[27] He quotes John Chrysostom for whom the altar "is an object of wonder: by nature it is stone, but it is made holy when it receives the body of Christ."[28] With the altar—understood as the definitive medium of God's self-sacrificial service—as the key focal point in the layout and ritual drama, the worshipping Church is more conscious of the reality by which she is drawn into communion with "the living stone, rejected by men but chosen by God and precious to him," from whom she derives her own identity as "a building of living stones . . . a holy priesthood, offering spiritual sacrifices acceptable to God through Jesus Christ" (1 Pet. 2:4–5).

The ancient Church made much of the eastward orientation of the church building and its sacrificial liturgical acts. East was the place of the primordial paradise (Gen. 2:8) from whence the risen

24 Josef Pieper, *Problems of Modern Faith: Essays and Addresses*, trans. Jan van Heurck (Chicago: Franciscan Herald Press, 1985), 102.

25 John W. Kleinig, *Leviticus* (Saint Louis: Concordia, 2003), 62–3.

26 Pieper, *Problems of Modern Faith*, 103.

27 Steven J. Schloeder, *Architecture in Communion: Implementing the Second Vatican Council through Liturgy and Architecture* (San Francisco: Ignatius, 1998), 63.

28 Schloeder, *Architecture in Communion*, 63.

Lord, "the sun of righteousness," would return to save (Mal. 4:2). For Origen it was perfectly clear that "we should make our prayers facing east, since this is a symbolic expression of the soul's looking for the rising of the true Light."[29] Referring to the physical "about-face" from west to east made by neophytes following the renunciation in the baptismal liturgy, Cyril of Jerusalem further explained:

> When, therefore, you renounce Satan, utterly breaking all covenant with him, that ancient league with hell, there is opened to you the Paradise of God, which he planted toward the East, whence for his transgression our first father was exiled; and symbolic of this was your turning from the West toward the East, the place of light.[30]

Again, for the Fathers, facing east was not considered to be an incidental detail, whether for individual or corporate prayer. For them it held a fundamentally christological meaning: to face east was to align oneself to Christ, man's true light and "origin" (*arche*) of the cosmos. Today the consciousness of this prophetism of the liturgical body has largely been lost. Since the advent of electricity, societies which formerly ordered their daily activities, including worship, in conscious harmony with the rhythms of the sun, the moon, and the seasons of the earth have been enabled to determine new habits according to functional requirements. Yet a recovery of the sense of worship as a performative act involving the whole cosmos is possible. As Ratzinger once commented:

> We . . . need to be reminded that liturgy involves the cosmos—that Christian liturgy is cosmic liturgy. In it we pray and sing in concert with everything "in heaven and earth and under the earth" (Phil. 2:10), we join in with the praise rendered by the sun and the stars. Thus in church architecture, for instance, we should see to it that churches are not designed merely with human utility in mind, but that they

29 Origen, *On Prayer* 32.
30 Cyril of Jerusalem, *Mystagogic Catecheses* 1, 9.

stand in the cosmos, inviting the sun to be a sign of the praise of God and a sign of the mystery of Christ for the assembled community. A rediscovery of the value of the church building's eastward orientation would help . . . in recovering a spirituality which embraces the dimension of creation.[31]

Much more could be said on the topic of ritual topography, including the negative impact of the self-enclosing orientation of priest and people, and of the introduction of a multitude of technological "aids" such as microphones and power-point screens.[32] But it will suffice to adduce a few brief insights drawn from the mystagogical theology of Maximus the Confessor in which the metaphysical and theological importance of ritual topography again comes to the fore. Maximus discerned in the twofold division of the liturgical space into nave and sanctuary a concrete analogy of simultaneous unity and diversity in Christ, the Church, the human being, and the cosmos. The integrity of each "part" is constituted by its "reference" (*anaphora*) to the whole, a reference performatively enacted by means of the unfolding ritual drama.[33] The sanctuary, towards which the focus of the people in the nave is drawn and to which they finally come for holy communion, constitutes the culminating destination of the whole liturgy. The two spaces in the church building are thus distinct elements in a single "entity" (*hypostasis*) whose final, subjective singularity is brought about by the ordered, reciprocal penetration of its parts and their ritually determined orientation to their final state. Both the topography and the ritual action are determinative in God's action of drawing the distinct members of the Church together to make them in fact what they potentially

31 Joseph Cardinal Ratzinger, *The Feast of Faith* (San Francisco: Ignatius, 1986), 143.

32 In an observation by German sociologist and psychoanalyst Alfred Lorenzer, "The whole scene is more reminiscent of the studio setup for a television cooking show." Quoted by Klaus Gamber, *The Reform of the Roman Liturgy: Its Problems and Background*, trans. Klaus D. Grimm (California: Una Voce Press, 1993), 171.

33 Maximus the Confessor, *Mystagogy* 2.

are: the new creation, the body of Christ, the deified cosmos.[34] In contrast to Dionysius the Areopagite, whose liturgical theology lacks any kind of eschatological trajectory, the ritually achieved ecclesial union Maximus envisages between God and the cosmos is nothing short of the future nuptial mystery,

> the blessed and most holy intercourse by virtue of which there is accomplished that awesome mystery of the union surpassing mind and reason, a mystery through which God becomes one flesh and one spirit with the Church, and thus with the soul, and the soul with God.[35]

Thus the Church is the deified, deifying reality she is precisely through and, in this age, never apart from, her theandric interpersonal ritual actuation in a defined space before an altar.

---

34 See Cooper, *The Body in Saint Maximus*, 190–205.
35 Maximus the Confessor, *Mystagogy* 5.

3

Sign and Symbol

IT IS NOT my intention in this chapter to attempt anything approaching an analysis of semiotic or symbolic theory. My goal is far more modest. Stopping far short of a detailed interpretation of specific liturgical signs, I want instead to ask what the concept of sign means for liturgical theology, insofar as the liturgy may be described as a system of ritual signs. This seems an important preliminary step in the formulation of a liturgical theology of the body. For central to a theology of the body is the conviction that creation as a whole constitutes a visible and sacramental sign of the hidden mystery of God. This is all the more true in the case of the sexually differentiated human body, since human beings, as male and female, are created according to the image and likeness of God. Precisely in this unique quality, as John Paul II has stated, the human body "is capable of making visible what is invisible: the spiritual and the divine. It has been created to transfer into the visible reality of the world the mystery hidden from eternity in God, and thus to be a sign of it."[1] Since the human bodily structure is intrinsically revelatory and pregnant with nuptial sacramental promise, the term "sign" would seem to possess a vital function also in a liturgical theology of the body.

Liturgy and Signs

Some might question whether the term "sign" is altogether an appropriate category in a liturgical theology. Aidan Kavanagh, for example, has argued that ritual should be understood as a sys-

---

1 TOB, 203.

tem of symbols rather than what he deems "mere signs." Signs, he charges, are too unambiguous, too objective, and too direct. "Symbols," by contrast,

> being roomy, allow many different people to put them on, so to speak, in different ways. . . . Symbols coax one into a swamp of meaning and require one to frolic in it. Symbol is rarely found among the inactive, the obtuse, the confused, or the dull. Signs are to symbols what infancy is to adulthood, what stem is to flower, and the flowering of maturity takes time.[2]

However I suspect Kavanagh is somewhat overstating the difference in meaning between sign and symbol. Is not the level of ambiguity or fluidity attached to a sign or symbol dependent upon its intention and use? Chauvet defines a symbolic order as a system of connections "forming a coherent whole that allows the social group and individuals to orient themselves in space, find their place in time, and in general situate themselves in the world in a significant way," at the same time acknowledging Lévi-Strauss's assertion that "there always remains an inexpungible residue of signifiers to which we can never give adequate meanings."[3]

Just as language can be defined and employed in a variety of ways, from the simple "signs" of animal communication to the profound "symbols" of human poetry, so it seems can the external words, images, and actions of the liturgy be variously intended and construed. At one extreme, where the liturgy has become an entirely didactic affair, even "symbols" can be emptied of mystery and depth and reduced to pedagogical aids. At the other end of the scale lies Kavanagh's "swamp of meaning" which, leaving interpretation even of "signs" entirely to the subjectivity of the individual, seems just as problematic. Kavanagh's neat opposition of sign and symbol seems to overlook the flexibility of the terms in customary usage. The Church's creed has always been called a "symbol" without in any way suggesting its

---

2 Aidan Kavanagh, *Elements of Rite: A Handbook of Liturgical Style* (Collegeville, Minnesota: Liturgical Press, 1990), 5.

3 Chauvet, *Symbol and Sacrament*, 84–5.

contents lack some objective referent, while the "sign" (*sphragis*) of the cross has always provided an inexhaustible spring of meaning for subjective construction and interpretation.

Rather than drawing a sharp division between liturgical signs and symbols, it may be more helpful to understand both as "images through which ultimate metaphysical realities and modes of being are apprehended, not in an abstract manner but by way of likeness."[4] While this definition would unlikely meet the approval of more post-modern liturgiologists, it nonetheless preserves their concern for the notion of mediation and the inherent connection between the symbolic and language (with the latter being understood more as *event* than "pure" signifier). If we accept the meaning of poetry in its etymological sense, that is, as a creative art in language, then the liturgy, understood as a performative divine drama, has a place for both "signs" and "symbols" as poetic, creative forms.

Accepting this approach as legitimate, a liturgical theology of the body can concern itself with signs for a number of reasons, not least of which is the fact that in the liturgy communion with God is lived and mediated bodily, that is, by means of signs. While it is the nature of signs in general to function as witnesses to or representations of the real, it is the special quality of the primary liturgical signs—linguistic, ritual, and material—to function as constitutive of the real. They are not just "revealers" but eventful "operators."[5] This is not to deny their intrinsically metaphorical, even provisional character, nor to overlook their historical particularity, the fact that their meaning is constituted by factors specific to tradition, community, and culture. But in keeping with a sacramental and theological realism, and against any sort of Christian empiricism, a liturgical theology of the body insists that this contextuality does not deprive the primary liturgical signs of their transcendent, "referential status."[6] As Dionysius

4 Gertrud von le Fort, *The Eternal Woman: The Timeless Meaning of the Feminine*, trans. Marie Cecilia Buehrle (San Francisco: Ignatius, 2010), 3.

5 See Chauvet, *Symbol and Sacrament*, 544.

6 See Janet Martin Soskice, *Metaphor and Religious Language* (Oxford: Clarendon Press, 1987), 142–61.

the Areopagite discerned, the revelatory efficacy of signs that are altogether *unlike* their referents is in no way diminished simply because those referents are supernatural. Rather, the unlikeness between sign and signed all the more correctly discloses the truth that the mysteries in which the Church is actually caught up are ultimately transcendent and beyond being.

Sign and Typology

Having said that, the function of signs and symbolism in the liturgy cannot be limited to static representation, nor to performative efficacy. Something subjective and constructive is also at work. Insight can be gained by drawing an analogy between the functions of sign in the liturgy and the anagogical dimension of the scriptural text as understood in patristic and medieval exegesis. In his substantial study of traditional Christian biblical hermeneutics, Henri de Lubac has identified two dimensions of the anagogical reading of sacred Scripture: one "objective and doctrinal," the other pertaining to "its subjective realization."[7] The first unveils intelligible realities; the second brings those realities into the here and now. Applying this schema to the drama of the liturgy, signs are not only to be taken allegorically and vertically, as constitutive representations of objective metaphysical realities, but also tropologically and horizontally, as dynamic, unfolding modes of historic and subjective participation in the eternal inheritance of the life to come.

This application of anagogical hermeneutics to the liturgy seems congruent with the typological dynamics of God's own dealings with his people in the drama of salvation history. A brief exegetical excursus may help bring this aptness to light. Throughout God's dealings with his people of the old covenant, and particularly in the ritual confirmation of various covenants, a vital function was attributed to the sign (*'ôth*). Usually translated in the Septuagint as *semeion*, the Hebrew word *'ôth* often refers simply to a miracle or supernatural wonder performed by God to manifest

---

7 See Henri de Lubac, *Medieval Exegesis,* vol. 2, trans. Marc Sebanc (Grand Rapids: Eerdmans, 1998), 179–87.

his power or to confirm his determined and express will. Most uses of the term indicate it to be an object meant to be perceived by the senses, especially to sight.[8] So in Genesis 9:12–16, the rainbow functions as the sign of the Noahide covenant, a visual sign intended primarily for God himself: "Whenever the rainbow appears in the clouds, I will see it and I will remember the everlasting covenant between God and all living creatures. . ." (9:16). The sign here prompts a kind of performative *anamnesis* on God's part by which the pledged benefits of the covenant are brought to bear on its recipients anew. A similar function seems to be accorded to other visual and covenantal signs, including circumcision (Gen. 17:10–11), the blood of the Passover lamb (Ex. 12:12–13), and the Sabbath (Ex. 31:13). In each case, the sign calls for mutual recognition by both the divine and human members of the covenant, somehow establishing and confirming their covenantal union.

In the commissioning of Moses by God in Exodus 4:1–17, we have an example where the visual character of the sign is joined by an aural character as well. Here Yahweh gives to Moses the power to perform certain "signs"—changing his staff to a snake and making his hand leprous—which are to function for both the Egyptians and the Israelites as validating signals or demonstrations of Moses' divine authorization: "This is so that they may believe that Yahweh, the God of their fathers . . . has appeared to you" (Ex. 4:5). Yet the Hebrew in this pericope indicates more than a visual aspect to the sign. It possesses an aural quality as well: if the people will not heed "the voice" of Moses, they should at least heed "the voice of the sign" (LXX: *tes phones tou semeiou*). This curious construct gives us reason to invoke an analogy of attribution: while materially visual, the sign appears nevertheless to "speak" with its own voice, or rather, with the voice of God.[9]

---

8 See the section on 'ôth as an object of sense perception in Rolf Rengstorf, "semeion," in Kittel, ed., *Theological Dictionary of the New Testament*, vol. 7, 211–13.

9 On the "analogy of attribution," see TOB, 542. As there is no instance of the 'ôthoth speaking in the OT, as Rengstorf notes (op. cit., 212), this curious combination of the verb "to hear" with 'ôth as the object seems to stand out as all the more unusual, and therefore worthy of attention.

The combination of '*ôth* with the verb "to remember" (*zacar*), already anticipated in the Noahide covenant mentioned above, seems to also be of significance in other settings. In Exodus 13:9, the terms "sign" and "remembrance" are virtually synonymous. The observance of the Passover will be for the people of Israel "like a sign on your hand and a remembrance on your forehead." In Deuteronomy 7:18–19, Moses exhorts the people to "remember" the mighty acts of the Lord in Egypt, visible to all in "the great trials, the miraculous signs and wonders" with which the Lord delivered them. What is striking here though is that the addressees in question are not the first generation who were delivered from Egypt, who all died during the long wilderness wanderings, but their second and third generation offspring. Yet to these people Moses can say with reference to those original signs, "You saw [them] *with your own eyes. . . .*" It is as though the original (visual) signs, from which the people in the here and now are separated in time, are made effectively present in the (oral/aural/ritual) remembrance of them. The signs effect certain knowledge and faith by their performative "remembrance," which in biblical theology is as much a physical and performative activity as it is mental and recollective. The enactment of certain "signs" by the prophets seems to confirm this same kind of causal connection, though in a future-oriented direction. Isaiah's going about naked for three years functions as a performative "sign" heralding the impending humiliation of Egypt and the countries of the Upper Nile under the Assyrian superpower (Is. 20:1–6). Ezekiel's war game with mud and sticks functions as a performative sign heralding the impending siege and collapse of Jerusalem (Ez. 4:1–3). Such signs, gaining their historical efficacy as Yahweh's visual speech-acts, do not merely predict the future, but embody it *in nuce* and effectively accomplish it ahead of time.

From the perspective of the new covenant, all the signs of salvation history mentioned so far possess a provisional, typological character in relation to the ultimate covenantal sign, the incarnate Word. From his birth, Christ is the sign that all the world's hopes for a Saviour are now fulfilled (Lk. 2:12). The demand for a sign *from* Jesus signals a blindness to the sign that he is and will be in his death, resurrection, and *parousia* (Mt. 12:38; 16:1; 24:30). In John's Gospel we notice a co-ordination of the demonstrative, visual signs of Jesus' works with the interpretative, aural signs of his words. Both come from the Father; both aim at arousing faith and communicating divine life; both culminate in Christ's glorification. According to C.H. Dodd, the signs of Jesus disclose "timeless realities."[10] Yet many saw his works, heard his words, and did not believe: "Man is too attached to his view and his own standards, and judges everything, man and God, as it is written, "according to the flesh" (8:15) or, "by appearances" (7:24).[11] The real meaning and life-giving content of the signs only breaks open to subjective self-surrender, to the hearing and seeing of faith.

A striking passage in Augustine's *De Trinitate* is especially illuminating in this regard, in which he comments on the role of subjective desire in the progressive understanding of the sign.[12] For Augustine, knowledge is the fruit of desire and love, for only by lovingly giving oneself to an object can one really know it. Yet this immediately raises a problem. For the fact is, "nothing can be loved unless it is known."[13] One cannot give oneself to something if it is not known in some way. But how then can God be loved, since in this life it is impossible to know him as he is?

The answer, says Augustine, is through the sign. For while nothing can be loved unless it is known, something can be loved, even if unknown, precisely through its sign, inasmuch as the sign is a promise of, even an incipient encounter with, the signified reality. Every sign engenders a desire on the part of the subject to know more perfectly that which the sign signifies. This desire in turn leads to true knowledge of and union with the reality. Thus, if we happened to encounter some sensible object or sound, but did not know it to be a sign, we would ignore it, and seek nothing further. But if we understood that object or sound to be a sign *of*

10 C.H. Dodd, *The Fourth Gospel* (Cambridge: Cambridge University Press, 1958), 142.

11 Heinrich Schlier, *The Relevance of the New Testament*, trans. W.J. O'Hara (London: Burns and Oates, 1968), 170.

12 Augustine, *On the Trinity* 10, 1, 2.

13 Ibid.

something, our desire to seek that something would be aroused and not satisfied until we found it.

Michael Polanyi's theory of tacit knowledge confirms the coherence of Augustine's intuition on this point: "All explicit forms of reasoning . . . are impotent in themselves; they can operate only as the intellectual tools of man's tacit powers reaching toward the hidden meaning of things."[14] It is within particular signs or symbols that we find the "clues" to propel us forward to more comprehensive understanding of the unknown. As Polanyi writes,

> The task of solving a problem must indeed appear self-contradictory unless we admit that we can possess true intimations of the unknown. . . . [E]very advance in understanding is moved and guided by our power for seeing the presence of some hidden comprehensive entity behind yet incomprehensible clues pointing increasingly toward this yet unknown entity.[15]

For a liturgical theology of the body, this sheds light on the complex interplay of faith and subjective desire in apprehending the intelligible content of liturgical signs. While signs do not fully disclose the realities they signify, and may in fact largely conceal them, they still play a crucial role in the process by which full knowledge, through love, can eventually be realized. Nor are they mere accessories that can be replaced arbitrarily or done away with once given. Rather they are "structuring elements" critical to the shaping of faith-filled desire.[16] But that is precisely the point: without desire, there can be no knowledge. As Polanyi asserts, "Formal processes of inference cannot thrust toward the truth, for they have neither passion nor purpose."[17] Only signs, as mythopoeic symbolic forms saturated with the power to enchant, can engender the kind of desire crucial to the passage to the real.

---

14 Michael Polanyi, "Faith and Reason," *Journal of Religion* 41 / 4 (1961), 237–47, at 243.

15 Ibid.

16 See Chauvet, *Symbol and Sacrament*, 164.

17 Polanyi, "Faith and Reason," 243.

What meanings liturgical signs disclose, and how they are disclosed, depends in large part on such dynamic and variable conditions as personal experience and collective intentionality, both of which are influenced by subjective factors. There is a certain sense in which their intelligibility and coherence also depends on a minimum level of predictability, a collective recognition of them *as signs*. This interest in "intelligibility" should not be mistaken as an intellectualism alien to faith in the performative efficacy of the sacraments or opposed to affective participation in divine worship. On the contrary, if worship involves the suffering of divine beauty, and if beauty refers to the desired true and good as it appears to the intellect, then both aesthetic delight and spiritual cognition have their place. As Augustine discerns, recognition of signs as promissory forms—as anagogical types—is vital for arousing a certain kind of attractive desire. Similarly, when it comes to participating in ritual, one can only fully give oneself over—surrender in faith—to what one already knows, even if that knowing is incipient and partial. The capacity to discern a real, objective content to liturgical signs depends ultimately on their objective basis and origin in God and on their commensurability with the Spirit-inspired grammar of Christian faith. Learning to read liturgical signs in the truth, like learning to read the body in the truth, is both an art and vocation. The successful use of ritual depends in large part on successful initiation of participants into the transcultural world of the liturgy, on an increasing and eventually complete familiarity with the particular and external aspects of the rite, a familiarity in which those external aspects lose all opacity and become fully transparent to their true spiritual meaning and content.

Semitive Symbolics

The use of signs or external symbolic forms in the divine service corresponds to two pivotal facts: the humanization of the eternal Word of God, and the integral physicality of human beings. As a prolongation in time and space of the tangible mystery of Jesus the Christ, the liturgy stands between these two facts as a kind of mediating link. We need repeatedly to remind ourselves that the liturgy is not first of all a matter of texts and calendars and rubrics, but of physical enactment, and that it is through such physical action that the worshipping Church suffers divine things and so is joined to her divine head as a bride to her husband.

That this is possible is just because human bodies are persons, because human physical action is personal action, and therefore because the liturgy is also a profoundly personal, subjective encounter. The prayers and ritual gestures of the faithful are not simply magical formulas, nor are the word and sacraments conduits of some quasi-divine, impersonal force. In them is embodied an erotic and ecstatic interplay, a mutual giving and receiving between Christ, a divine-human person, one of the holy Trinity, and his own bride, a subsistent communion of persons. The Holy Spirit, active in the means of grace, is likewise a person. His interior operations in the hearts of the faithful are strictly personal, in the mode of an I-Thou, subject to subject relation. He does not violate personal freedom, nor does he magically coerce the human will from without. In the philosophical language of Thomas Aquinas, the Holy Spirit operates with formal causation in the human heart, but not with efficient causation.[18] Respecting the nature of the person as a self-determining being (*dominus sui*), the Spirit of Christ elicits a motion of the human will in such a way that the motion is self-caused, and therefore free, yet at the same time undeniably dependent upon the gracious initiative and the formally causative power of divine love. The liturgical deployment of signs as the primary mode of interaction must be understood and interpreted within the framework of this personal, intersubjective dynamic.

As an aspect of this subjective aspect, and in keeping with the fact that they belong to the symbolic order of matter and history, signs would seem to be essentially changeable realities. Just as language evolves through history, so that words acquire, change, or lose meaning depending on usage, so it would seem that signs, including liturgical signs, are essentially contingent, their normativity being imposed upon them by the particular communities in which they have meaning.

18 See ST I–II, 113, 3–8.

Yet alongside this recognition of the contingent character of signs we must also consider the possibility that there are some signs that possess a kind of permanent, archetypal status, and which are therefore not liable to resignification, whether by calculated revision or arbitrary manipulation.[19] Aquinas seemed to be aware of such higher order signs when, in expounding his exegetical principles, he spoke of a double signification: one through words, the other through the things signified by the words. Not only do the words of Scripture signify, but the things signified by those words also have their own unique signification.[20] It is not out of the question to suggest a similar dual order of signification going on in the system of signs that make up the Church's liturgy as well. Borrowing a term from C.S. Lewis, we may fittingly call such signs "semitive figures" which present themselves to us as "live and awful shadows of realities utterly beyond our control and largely beyond our direct knowledge."[21] Somehow transcending the symbolic order, while remaining within it, their immediate connection to what they signify is not constructed from without, nor a symptom of religious imagination or subjective creativity, but is an intrinsic feature native to their very constitution as divine signs. Such signs are recognized as being invested with significatory or symbolic value by the very fact of their given-ness by God, not as a consequence of cultural forces. Their signification therefore works more at the level of a pregnant and poetic actualisation of meaning, than simply at the level of a provisional and, in principle, substitutable, indication of meaning.

19 In one of the first forays into the body language of sexual intercourse, Paul M. Quay made use of the distinction between "the objective" and "intentional" orders of symbol and language. He remarked that whatever its "speakers" may wish or intend, sexual intercourse possesses an objective symbolism of interpersonal communion, which is not within the speakers' power to change. See Paul M. Quay, "Contraception and Conjugal Love," *Theological Studies* 22 (1961), 18–40, reprinted in Janet E. Smith (ed.), *Why Humanae Vitae Was Right: A Reader* (San Francisco: Ignatius, 1993), 19–45.

20 Thomas Aquinas, *Commentary on the Epistle to the Galatians* 4, 7.

21 See C.S. Lewis, *Undeceptions: Essays on Theology and Ethics*, ed. Walter Hooper (London: Geoffrey Bles, 1971), 191–6.

What I am talking about finds a certain analogy in J.R.R. Tolkien's notion of fairy stories as subcreation. True fairy stories must possess an "inner consistency of reality."[22] They must be derived from reality, participate in it, and flow towards it. In contrast to totemism or magic, which produces "an alteration in the Primary World," their symbolic forms permit "the very taste of primary truth."[23]

Like true fairy story or true myth, which for Tolkien is definitively epitomized in the "eucatastrophe" of the incarnation of the Son of God and his atoning redemption of mankind, the liturgy can be said to effect a symbolic subcreation, a dramatic myth. Its truthfulness and power to enchant, however, depends on its "inner consistency of reality," its fidelity in giving a taste of the "primary world" from which it derives it full meaning. For the liturgy really to unite heaven and earth, God to humanity, it cannot randomly adopt just any symbolic order, deploying signs whose meaning or intelligible content is constituted only by the subjective intention of the assembly or certain of its members. Rather it must rely in the main on a symbolic order where meaning is intrinsic to the signs themselves, objectively inscribed therein, through promise and institution, by their author.

What signs could possibly fulfil this description? The first obvious answer lies in the sacraments. Their intelligible "content'—that which they signify—is not arbitrarily invented by the assembly, but is proposed to the assembly by their author. Moreover, that meaning and content cannot be abstracted or separated from the constitutive ritual and material forms in which they are embodied. What they *are* at the level of their concrete, historically contingent symbolic specificity is intrinsically related to what they *mediate*, what they *signify*, at the level of spiritual and sacramental actualisation.

A second example, again crucial to the liturgy, can be found in certain revealed words, metaphors and divine names, including

22 J.R.R. Tolkien, *On Fairy-Stories*, eds. Verlyn Flieger and Douglas A. Anderson (London: Harper Collins, 2008), 59.

23 Ibid. See further Marc Sebanc, "J.R.R. Tolkien: Lover of the Logos," *Communio* 20 (1993), 84–106.

the revealed name of the holy Trinity. The words "Father," "Son," and "Holy Spirit" are not arbitrary signs whose signified "contents" can be equally mediated or rendered intelligible by alternative terms. Precisely in their ordered relationality and specificity, in their non-exchangeability for more generic, univocal terms of address, lies their theological and revelatory significance, their meaning and function as doxological and invocatory means of access to God.

A third example of an archetypal, semitive sign is the sexually differentiated human body. What the human body *is* at the level of its biological and sexually specific determinations is intrinsically related to what it *means*, what it *signifies*, at the level of its personal and moral actualisation. This is not to deny that "sexual meaning is a creative work of human reason,"[24] nor, in the way of some kind of biologistic naturalism, to suggest that it should be conceived "as some kind of pre-made substantial entity, enjoying a life of its own and independent from the real human subjects which give it existence."[25] But neither is human reason ever utterly independent of the material and historical conditions of its instantiation. Reason does not appear in the world without certain givens, within whose limits it must conduct its project of making meaning. The sexed body constitutes one of those limits, not in the negative sense of a restrictive, deterministic boundary, but in the positive sense of a trajectory already steeped in sense and purpose and direction. The only restriction the body presents is to a reason that would escape the physical, a reason that rejects the human and idolizes the angelic.

This means that within the scope of freedom proper to reason's construction of sexual meaning, fundamentally alternative meanings cannot be imposed upon or read into the sign of the body without distortion or violation of the minimum meaning that is already, intrinsically *there*. As I shall argue in the next chapter, this has immediate significance when it comes to the liturgy and in understanding the sign of the priesthood and the Church's

24 Andre Guindon, *The Sexual Language: An Essay in Moral Theology* (University of Ottawa Press, 1977), 37.
25 Ibid., 41.

feminine identity *vis a vis* Christ. For as John Paul II has argued, Scripture itself supplies the logic by which this sign or language of the sexual body is constituted as an intrinsic, even "absolute" dimension with respect to the signs or language of the liturgy, so that "the sacramental sign of marriage is built up in the language of the liturgy and in the whole liturgical ritual."[26]

26 TOB, 612.

4

Christ and Priest

A LITURGICAL THEOLOGY of the body must take seriously the essential continuity between the Jesus of history and the living Christ who, seated at the right of the Father in glory, hiddenly pervades the world with his bodily presence in the Church. The holy flesh of Christ, already interior to the Trinity, remains also the *locus deificandi* on earth, the divinely ordained meeting point of God and humanity.

At the same time, however, and notwithstanding certain dramatic and extraordinary events such as the Lord's epiphany in Paul's Damascus Road experience, we are struck by a certain alteration in the physical modality by which the incarnate Word makes himself available in the world following his resurrection and glorification. On the one hand, the Christ who broke bread with his disciples on the night of his betrayal is the same Christ who breaks bread with them on that first day of the week, confirming the continuity of his personal identity with specific reference to his body: "Look at my hands and feet. It is I myself! Touch me and see, a ghost does not have flesh and bones, as you see I have" (Lk. 24:39). On the other hand, the risen Lord exhibits bodily attributes that mark him out as somehow changed: locked doors do not hinder his entry; people see him but do not recognize him. Jesus' *"noli me tangere"* (Jn. 20:17) seems to belong to a wider pedagogical strategy on the part of the early Spirit-guided ecclesial community aimed at reconstituting the encounter with Jesus' glorified body in a new way. Communion with Jesus is to become more a liturgically mediated experience. Fellowship with Christ in the flesh is to be realized through fellowship with the apostolic college and acceptance of its testimony and ritual acts performed in Christ's name: "we proclaim to you what we have seen and heard, so that you also may have fellowship with us. And our fellowship is with the Father and with his Son, Jesus Christ" (1 Jn. 1:3). As Chauvet writes, "So you wish to know if Jesus is really living, he who is no longer visible before your eyes? . . . Live in the Church! It is there that you will discover and recognize him."[1]

Enfleshing the Logos

If this is true, then there follow vital implications for the order of the priestly and sacramental ministry, whose foundation lies not simply in the general priesthood of the baptized, nor in personal charisma, but in the high priestly ministry of Christ and in his personal institution of the apostolic office. The priest acts *in persona Christi*, which may best be translated not "in the person of Christ," a phrase whose meaning is not immediately intelligible, nor even "in the place of Christ" or "instead of Christ," which suggest standing in for one who is absent, but "with and for Christ," or even "as Christ." The priesthood is at once a christological, priestly, and apostolic office. To its incumbents Jesus says: "he who hears you hears me" (Lk. 10:16). Their liturgical service is directed towards the offering of a sacrifice: a people sanctified by the Holy Spirit (Rom. 15:16). When the risen Jesus appeared bodily to his chosen Apostles, he said: "Just as the Father has sent me, so also I send you." *Just as . . . so also*. In the same way also the successors of the Apostles participate in Christ's Spirit-filled, incarnate mission, so that what they do, he does in them: "If you forgive anyone his sins, they are forgiven. If you do not forgive them, they are not forgiven" (Jn. 20:21–22). And so Paul can speak of himself and his apostolic colleagues as "ambassadors for Christ," ministers of reconciliation, "with God as it were making his appeal through us" (2 Cor. 5:20).

This at least has been the way the priesthood has been understood from the earliest centuries. Maximus the Confessor represents the patristic consensus when he speaks of God having ordained the priesthood, which for the Confessor is a term inclusive of both the priestly and episcopal offices, "in order to repre-

---

1 Chauvet, *Symbol and Sacrament*, 166.

56

sent him on earth to ensure that he may not cease being seen bodily and that his mysteries may not cease appearing to those with eyes to see." The priesthood is "a visible representation of the blessed Godhead to those on earth," "a picture which in icon form suitably portrays what it represents."[2] Noteworthy in these quotations is the liturgical context within which these descriptions are situated, and the emphasis upon visibility and thereby on the body of the priest as a physical sign. Not that every baptized Christian does not embody Christ and bear his image; yet, as Thomas Aquinas notes, those endowed with the sacrament of orders are "assimilated to God in their own way as kind of co-operators with God."[3] As a special kind of *charaktêr* or *eikôn* or *typus* of Christ, the priest/bishop has been set apart to communicate heavenly, divine realities on earth bodily and visibly. For the Fathers the priest represents God as much to the eyes as to any other sense. While the apostolic office is a teaching office concerned with the administration of the holy mysteries and the proclamation of the powerful divine word, this oral and aural aspect of the ministry can be separated from the visual and physical aspect no more than the divinity of Christ can be separated from his humanity. That is why the physical entrance of the priest carries such ritual gravity in traditional liturgies. "Without his presence, the gathered assembly would not be the Church in the full sense of the word."[4] Word and sign, teaching and teacher, office and person, sacrament and priest: these things belong together.

Fatherhood and Sonship

If the priestly ministry of the word of God (objective genitive) is no less the personal ministry of the incarnate Word of God (subjective genitive), then the priest may be said to participate in a

---

2 These and other similar passages are collated in Cooper, *The Body in Saint Maximus the Confessor*, 169–73.

3 ST *suppl.* 34, 1.

4 David Bird, *The Royal Road to Joy: The Beatitudes and the Eucharist* (Chicago: Hillenbrand, 2003), 139.

unique way in the mediatorial ministry of Christ, the Son of God, one of the holy Trinity. Just as Jesus was aware of speaking not in his own name, but only in the name of his Father, so the Christian priest, in turn acting in the name of the bishop, "makes himself the voice of Christ" and, by enabling fellowship with the humanity of Jesus, draws the Christian assembly "into the dynamics of the trinitarian relationship."[5]

But if word and sign, office and person are indivisible, then it is similarly impossible to separate the liturgical and sacramental functions of the priesthood from the total somatic unity of the person of the priest, which of course includes his sexuality, a factor as deep as his genetic constitution. To say that the maleness of the priest, which goes "right down to each cell" of his body and affects his "whole empirical experience and ego-consciousness,"[6] is not incidental to his priestly office is to imply that Christ's maleness is not incidental to his redemptive office. The problem many of our contemporaries have in accepting the Church's reservation of priestly orders to men arises from conceiving the incarnation simply as a revelation of God-as-human in general, without reference to the specificity of Christ's male humanity and his order as only-begotten Son of the Father within the trinitarian relations. Some of course will argue that the orthodox credal tradition goes no further than asserting the Son's true humanity: "and became man" translates the Greek *enanthropesanta*, which contains only the generic word *anthropos* (human being), not *aner* (male). As Gregory Nazianzen declared, "What is not assumed is not healed."[7] Which some have taken to imply that, if Christ has only become male, and not fully human, and if this maleness is proposed as salvifically significant, then half of humanity lies outside the scope of his redemptive recapitulation.

But the present widespread confusion over sexuality calls us to go beyond the abstract and, in keeping with the biblical witness

5 Joseph Ratzinger, "The Ministry and Life of Priests," in *Pilgrim Fellowship of Faith: The Church as Communion*, trans. Henry Taylor (San Francisco: Ignatius, 2005), 153–75, at 160.

6 Balthasar, *Theodrama* 2, 364–5.

7 Gregory Nazianzen, *Epistle* 101, 32 (to Cledonius).

to the concrete, to recognize in Jesus the man the visible face not just of "God," but specifically of God the Father. This in fact is Jesus' own testimony: "Whoever has seen me, has seen the Father" (Jn. 14: 9), and "I and the Father are one" (Jn. 10:30). If we take seriously the inclusion of the bodily somehow in the *imago Dei*, that is, if our created embodiment as sexually differentiated persons expresses a language that—with a similarity enclosed within the ever greater dissimilarity proper to the *analogia entis*—signifies certain supernatural mysteries, then Christ's maleness should at the very least be acknowledged as somehow crucial in the redemptive plan, even if the specific reasons for it have not always been clear. It is only as the Church has had to grapple with alien theologies—whether associated with moves to ordain women or neutralize biblical and liturgical language or enculturate revealed truth or legitimate homosexual eroticism—that the ineliminable significance of Christ's maleness has become more apparent. As William Weinrich, responding to the christological question involved in the argument for women priests, discerns:

> Christ's flesh is not merely a dumb instrument, but is itself flesh of the Word and therefore it speaks, "Here is your Father. Whoever sees me sees the Father, for I and the Father are one." The flesh of Christ is the active source of that new life which the Father gives by begetting us anew. . . . Since God so created the human race that it would be the male member who can be father, to be male is by revelation the proper mode of the incarnate Son who brings and manifests the divine Father.[8]

Needless to say, the body-language by which Christ exercises this filial fatherhood embraces not domination, but submission, surrender, and self-sacrifice.

What then of the patristic adage cited earlier: what is not assumed is not healed? Can Christ authentically embrace the

8 William Weinrich, *It is not given to women to teach: A* lex *in search of a* ratio (Fort Wayne, Indiana: Concordia Theological Library Press, 1991), 28.

female sex within the limitations of his male humanity? Does not assigning theological significance to Jesus' maleness "qualify or deny the universality of his redemption"?[9]

Here one must not overlook the biblical depiction of the representative character of the Word's humanity, who was conceived and born precisely as "a male-child" (Rev. 12:5). Just as the first Adam contained Eve and gave her "birth" from his side, so the new Adam contains all humanity within himself, giving birth to her in the wounding of his side on the cross and the subsequent outpouring of the sacraments. As the new Eve, the Church, "designed to complement the man Christ, must come forth from within him, as his 'fullness' (Eph. 1:23)."[10] This also seems to be in keeping with the overall trajectory of salvation history. Reading the Old Testament typologically, we find fathers of households, high-priests, and first-born male animals summing up or containing within themselves the kinship communities whom they represent. In a similar way, precisely and only as a man, does Christ, "a lamb without blemish or defect" (1 Pet. 1:19), perfectly represent God the Father to all humanity, and unite all humanity to God. This also seems to be what is implied when the New Testament speaks of Christ as "head" (kephale), apart from whom there can be no true "recapitulation" (anakephalaiosis).[11]

Is this to say, in a way echoing the more misogynist strains in Hellenistic anthropology, that there is in fact only one sex, the male, and that femininity can only be defined by reference to masculinity? This charge has been levelled against Hans Urs von Balthasar's account of sexual specificity. Corinne Crammer writes, "I believe that despite his attempt to construct a two-sex theological anthropology . . . , ultimately Balthasar reproduces the one-sex model in which the normative human being is implicitly male and

9 R.A. Norris, "The Ordination of Women and the 'Maleness' of Christ," *Supplementary Series of the Anglican Theological Review* 6 (June 1976), 69–80, at 74.

10 Hans Urs von Balthasar, *Theo-Drama: Theological Dramatic Theory, vol. 3: The Dramatis Personae: The Person in Christ*, trans. Graham Harrison (San Francisco: Ignatius, 1992), 284.

11 See Eph. 1:10; 4:15; 5:23; 1 Cor. 11:3; Col. 1:18.

Woman's definition is based around Man. . . ."[12] Of course, one could answer that the terms "male" and "female" involve co-ordinate, complementary concepts: neither makes sense without reference to the other.

But ultimately the issue turns on the ecclesiological and christological question of whether or not the Church really is from Christ. An affirmative answer in no way implies a negation or cancelling out of the fact that Christ is of Mary, and man born of woman. But it does recognize the absolute uniqueness of Christ's priesthood in that it flows directly from his inward divine Sonship. In her "yes," Mary archetypally represents humanity to God, but she does not represent God to humanity, nor can she speak the words *"hoc est corpus meum"* or *"ego te absolvo,"* for, as Balthasar points out, "[t]hese words can be meaningfully said only when the one pronouncing them represents *another*."[13] It is not only in his priestly functions, but also in his male flesh, that the priest represents the absolute otherness we meet in the enfleshed Word: his eternal paternal origin and transcendent mode of generation. We may fittingly conclude this section, and anticipate the next, with another of Balthasar's keen observations:

> The institution [of the priesthood] guarantees the perpetual presence of Christ the Bridegroom for the Church, his Bride. So it is entrusted to men who, though they belong to the overall feminine modality of the Church, are selected from her and remain in her to exercise their office; their function is to embody Christ, who comes to the Church to make her fruitful.[14]

12 Corinne Crammer, "One sex or two? Balthasar's theology of the sexes," in *The Cambridge Companion to Hans Urs von Balthasar*, eds. Edward T. Oakes and David Moss, (Cambridge: Cambridge University Press, 2004), 93–112, at 102.

13 Hans Urs von Balthasar, "Thoughts on the Priesthood of Women," *Communio* 23 (1996), 701–9, at 708.

14 Balthasar, *Theodrama* vol. 3, 354. For more detailed responses to the question of women's ordination see Sara Butler, *The Catholic Priesthood and Women: A Guide to the Teaching of the Church* (Chicago: Hillenbrand Books, 2007); Guy Mansini, "On Affirming a Dominical Intention of a Male Priesthood," *The*

Virginity and Nuptiality

With these comments, we are better positioned to consider the way the priest in his state of consecrated celibacy relates nuptially with the Church, both local and universal, to which he is bound in a liturgically constituted bond of love. We may begin by citing the strange paradox, articulated by John Paul II in his comments on Jesus' teaching about the non-existence of marriage in the future resurrection (Mt. 22:30), that the spousal meaning of the human body will only completely be manifested when it is ful-filled in the virginal state of all bodies of believers in the eschaton.[15] Restated here in a novel way is the notion, believed by the early Church to have been embodied by Christ himself and witnessed to in the New Testament, that human marriage is a relative state when compared to the more final, absolute voca-tion of virginity, in which both personal subjectivity and divine-human communion is most perfectly anticipated and eventually fulfilled.

How is this possible? How can the celibate vocation—and let us focus here particularly on the celibate priesthood—how can this mode of apparently solitary physical existence be said to anticipate the perfect nuptial intersubjectivity to be enjoyed in the resurrection more fully than the two-in-one-flesh bi-subjec-tive experience of married persons? How can one affirm the fact that at the beginning, the maker made human beings male and female, blessed them with a fruitful one flesh union, and ratified their union as indissoluble; yet at the same time affirm, as a truth about the same human subjects, that their final perfection will involve no giving or taking in marriage, but rather an existence more akin to physical virginity? Does this not involve the denial of "the beginning," the loss of the body's spousal meaning, the undoing of man's calling and fruitfulness as male and female?

To these pressing questions John Paul proposes an answer in

Thomist 61/2 (1997), 301–16; Manfred Hauke, *Women in the Priesthood? A System-atic Analysis in the Light of the Order of Creation and Redemption*, trans. David Kipp (San Francisco: Ignatius, 1988).

15 TOB, 395.

which he indicates that the human calling is to participate in a communion of persons at a more fundamental level than that of the human marital sphere. He writes:

> Marriage and procreation do not definitively determine the original and fundamental meaning of being a body nor of being, as a body, male and female. Marriage and procreation only give concrete reality to that meaning in the dimensions of history. The resurrection indicates the closure of the historical dimension.[16]

John Paul is careful to point out that this does not mean that the spousal meaning of the body will be lost or superseded. Such an inference would be to deprive the resurrected state of its proper physicality and continuity with created reality. Rather he wants his readers to envisage a "completely new experience," in no way alien to man's original or historical experiences, in which each person finds "in his glorified body the fountain and freedom of the gift," and with that gift "also all the communion that will constitute the great community of the communion of saints."[17] It is this same new experience to which Pope Paul VI seemed to be pointing when, having praised the high dignity of the sacrament of marriage, he spoke of "a new way" opened by Christ "in which the human creature, adhering totally and directly to the Lord, and preoccupied solely with him and his affairs, manifests in a clearer and more complete manner the profoundly innovatory reality of the New Testament."[18]

It may be asked whether the historical evolution of the doctrine of priestly celibacy has always been so clearly-focused upon the positive graces attached to the charism of celibacy "for the sake of the Kingdom." Due to circumstances of history and context, the numerous rulings in the early Church requiring deacons, priests and bishops to abstain from spousal intercourse before serving at the altar seem to leave the Church's requirements in this regard open to the charge of being tinged with an unhealthy fear of ritual

16 Ibid., 399.
17 Ibid., 400.
18 *Sacerdotalis caelibatus* (1967) §20.

contamination or moral defilement associated with the sexual act. In AD 385, for example, in addressing the situation in Spain in which married priests were found to be continuing in normal marital relations even while offering the sacrament on a daily basis, Pope Siricius stipulated permanent continence, that is, the total cessation of all sexual relations between clergy and their lawful spouses, as the "indissoluble" rule, citing as authority both levitical and apostolic precedents.[19] While in 390 the famous decree from the Council of Carthage names "purity," "perfect chastity," "perfect continence," and "all simplicity" as those necessary qualities of the clergy in the service of the sacraments that are somehow compromised by marital intercourse.[20]

But do these rulings, which Cochini identifies as the first in the Church's history to clarify "the Church's precise discipline with respect to clerical continence,"[21] indicate an insidious Manichean or Encratist piety that deserves repudiation and correction? Later clarifications clearly improve upon earlier expressions, explicitly excluding any depreciation of marriage, at the same time underscoring the fact that virginity is not demanded of the priesthood by its nature.[22] Yet to understand the rulings of the early Church within their proper context we need to return not only to the Fathers' keen sense of the solemn responsibilities of the priesthood, but also to their understanding of three things: 1) the need for undivided devotion for effective priestly service; 2) the christological nature of the priestly office; and 3) the eschatological meaning of voluntary continence for the sake of the Kingdom. The Fathers discerned in the first of these the relation between celibacy and undistracted devotion to God, a principle they saw prefigured in the Old Testament, embodied by Christ, and confirmed by the Apostle Paul (1 Cor. 7:32–35). As Cochini remarks:

---

19 See Christian Cochini, *The Apostolic Origins of Priestly Celibacy,* trans. Nelly Marans (San Francisco: Ignatius, 1990), 8–13.

20 Ibid., 3–7.

21 Ibid., 17.

22 See The Decree of the Second Vatican Council, *Presbyterorum Ordinis* (1965) §16; Paul VI, *Sacerdotalis caelibatus* (1967) §17; also more generally John Paul II, *Pastores dabo vobis* (1992).

the priests' perseverance in prayer is the safe guarantee of the multitudes' salvation. One could not conceive of a higher responsibility. The whole theology of the altar service will be governed by this principle. And the obligation of chastity appears as an indispensable corollary.[23]

Of this and the other two points, much more could be said. But let us try to draw together some final comments which will allow us to connect the long tradition of priestly celibacy to our reflections on performative nuptiality.

Among the numerous details of Christ's life that theology has never written off as an incidental detail is the fact that he never married. This stands in stark contrast to contemporary Jewish rabbinic, priestly, and social traditions which regarded marriage as a religiously privileged state. Perhaps Jesus could have married; by prevailing cultural standards, he should have married. Yet he did not. Considering Jesus' remarkably counter-cultural estimation of and positive interaction with women, and above all, his radical teaching on the indissolubility of marriage (Mk. 10:1–12) and "the ethos of the heart" (Mt. 5:27–30), his reasons could not have been anti-marital. Rather, the new humanity to which he wanted to give birth was to be the offspring of a spiritual generation by the imperishable seed of his teaching, "the living and enduring word of God" (1 Pet. 1:23). In his most intimate encounters with women, Jesus makes it clear that what he has to give them is of an eternal, gratuitous order (Lk. 7:36–50; Jn. 4:10; 8:1–11; 20:10–17).

As a crucial dimension of his divine mission, then, Jesus' celibacy has its ultimate source in the trinitarian communion, particularly in the original love of the Father.[24] Of this communion, which is not closed but open to the world which it has generated, the Son enters history as the incarnate mediator. Had Jesus married, he would necessarily have been bound to a woman in a mode of loving union which, of its very nature, excludes all rivals.

---

23 Cochini, *The Apostolic Origins of Priestly Celibacy*, 251.

24 See Marc Cardinal Ouellet, "Priestly ministry at the service of ecclesial communion," *Communio* 23 (1996), 677–87.

Precisely in his physical virginity, Jesus witnessed bodily to his total availability for all, to his supreme freedom, as Son of the Father, to be "all things to all people." In this way, far from isolating or alienating him from his followers, Jesus' celibacy made him

> able to enjoy the greatest closeness to every man, woman, and child. He was in a position to be the man for all. . . . In his human behavior he was able to reveal the total openness of the Father's heart, the divine love which is impartial in its universal scope and goes out equally to all.[25]

So it seems that the more perfectly the ministerial priesthood is to realize Christ's priestly office, according to which the Son offered himself in unreserved sacrifice to the Father on behalf of his bride and opened his Father's heart of love to the world, the more it must embody Christ's self-sacrificial love and his spiritual mode of engendering new life, and this in a regularized mode of physical life. In *Pastores dabo vobis*, John Paul refers repeatedly to the way the priest has been "configured" to Christ in a special way through the sacrament of holy orders, how he "resembles" Christ "the head and shepherd, the servant and spouse of the Church" (§3), and how he is "a living and transparent image of Christ the priest" (§12). Citing the Preface of the Liturgy of the Chrism Mass, John Paul describes the priestly vocation in terms of leading God's holy people in love, nourishing them by his word, and strengthening them through the sacraments (§15), terms exactly corresponding to Christ's spousal office in which he "loved the Church and gave himself up for her to make her holy, cleansing her through the washing with water through the word" (Eph. 5:25–26). As witness to Christ's spousal love, the priest is "called to live out Christ's spousal love toward the Church, his bride."

> [H]e must be capable of loving people with a heart which is new, generous and pure—with genuine self-detachment, with full, constant and faithful dedication and at the same

---

25 Jean Galot, *Theology of the Priesthood* (San Francisco: Ignatius, 1985), 231. See also the section "Celibacy and Prayer" in André Louf, *Teach Us to Pray*, trans. Hubert Hoskins (London: Darton, Longman and Todd, 1974), 63–8.

time with a kind of "divine jealousy" (cf. 2 Cor. 11:2) and even with a kind of maternal tenderness. . . . (§22)

In this way his continence for the sake of the Kingdom is "a sign and stimulus of love" and "a singular source of spiritual fertility in the world" (§29). Thus the priestly office is an *amoris officium*, whose "highest realization" is the celebration of the eucharist, the earthly consummation of human and trinitarian communion (§23). Because he is not only "in" the Church but also stands "before" the Church and, in some way, especially through his celebration of the eucharist, can be said to assemble and "constitute" the Church, the priest physically and personally represents the absolute primacy of the Father's regenerative salvific grace, given to the world in the flesh of the Son. Through his teaching and sacramental ministry especially, to which he is related not just functionally but ontologically and morally, the priest exercises a divine paternity issuing in a spiritual progeny and culminating in a proleptic nuptial union of Church and Christ, body and head, world and God, a paternity and nuptial union most unambiguously and prophetically testified to by his own configuration to the coming bridegroom in consecrated virginity.

And paradoxically, inasmuch as "the one and only key for understanding the sacramentality of marriage is the spousal love of Christ for the Church,"[26] priestly celibacy at once offers a counter-cultural affirmation of marriage and a unique witness to supernatural life in the resurrection. The priest who, embracing his virginity for the sake of the Kingdom, faithfully exercises his *amoris officium*, bears profound witness to that which is most lasting and personal in the conjugal vocation. He becomes an icon for both married and unmarried, women and men, of that trinitarian, creative, and kenotic love which history has encountered definitively in our Lord Jesus Christ.

26 TOB, 442.

.

5

Word and Prayer

IN PREVIOUS CHAPTERS I have emphasized the symbolic and visual dimension of liturgical action. In this chapter the focus is primarily on the oral and aural means of divine and human communion, especially through the public reading and preaching of the word of God. Following in the wake of several decades of widespread liturgical *ressourcement* and renewal,[1] the *Constitution on the Sacred Liturgy* promulgated by the Fathers of the Second Vatican Council not only stipulated a more prominent place in liturgical celebrations for the reading of the holy Scriptures, especially in the vernacular.[2] It also called for a renewal in the ministry of preaching, whose "character should be that of a proclamation of God's wonderful works in the history of salvation, that is, the mystery of Christ, which is ever made present and active within us, especially in the liturgy."[3] We have grown accustomed to dividing the mass into two parts: the liturgy of the word and the liturgy of the sacrament. But there is a sense in which this is an arbitrary and even false division; for while formally the word is indeed most noticeably read, sung, and proclaimed in the first part, the eucharistic sacrifice and communion constitute no less a proclamation of the *mirabilia Dei*, a thankful *homologia* by which we "proclaim Christ's death until he comes in

---

1 See, for example, the published version of papers given by such figures as Daniélou, von Balthasar, Bouyer, and Gelineau at the Third National Congress of the *Centre de Pastorale Liturgique* in Strasbourg (1958), in *The Liturgy and the Word of God* (Collegeville, Minnesota: The Liturgical Press, 1959).

2 *Sacrosanctum concilium* (1963) §35–6.

3 Ibid., §35.

glory."[4] In the judgement of Louis Bouyer, "it is impossible, without misunderstanding and tending to distort the very reality of the Catholic Church, to separate in fact the proclamation of the Word of God and sacramental life."[5]

It is no surprise then that the vitality of the Church's prayer life is likewise immediately correlative to her "warm and living love" for the word of God.[6] Prayer springs from an interior motion in the heart, directed ultimately to the Father, whose origin and cause is none other than the Spirit-filled word of God. Prayer is the echo of God's own voice in the heart. To pray is to share in the life of the Triune God, that is, to do theology, and the soul of theology is the word of God.[7] Prayer is essentially doxological discourse, "the mysterious but deliberate entry in the Spirit of a human being—in communion with the saints—into the eternal dialogue of the only-begotten Son with the immortal Father."[8] This "deliberate entry" is another way of referring to faith, that loving and hopeful surrender born from "hearing the word of Christ" (Rom. 10:17), a Pauline idea with two dimensions. The first involves an external, sensible encounter with the enfleshed Logos, whose living voice is heard in the gospel enacted, heard, and read. The second involves an internal, Spirit-inspired mental and affective grasping of the meaning and content of the proclaimed word. It goes without saying that only the second of these two dimensions constitutes saving Christian faith. Yet the second presupposes the first: no one can believe unless he hears, and no one hears unless someone preaches to him (Rom. 10:14–15). The inner hearing of faith, from which prayer springs, implies some kind of external bodily encounter with the word of God. Its

---

4 See A.M. Roquet, "The Whole Mass Proclaims the Word of God," in *The Liturgy and the Word of God*, 67–83.

5 Louis Bouyer, "The Word of God Lives in the Liturgy," in *The Liturgy and the Word of God*, 53–66, at 53.

6 *Sacrosanctum concilium* (1963) §24.

7 Cf. Evagrius Ponticus, *Chapters on Prayer* 60: "If you are a theologian you truly pray. If you truly pray you are a theologian"; also *Dei verbum* (1965) §24: "The study of the 'sacred page' ought to be the soul of sacred theology."

8 Cooper, "Christ as Teacher of Theology," 1053.

birth is effected "when a word or testimony coming from without intersects with the internal energies that dwell within."[9]

The Bodily Word

The liturgy, of course, is saturated with this bodily word. All the prayers, the readings, the acclamations, the hymns, the homily, the creed, the greetings and dialogues, are deeply rooted in the Church's Scriptures, always echoing and alluding to them, if not always explicitly quoting them. In them we hear God speaking. From them the physical actions and signs derive their meaning.[10] And as we have asserted repeatedly, God's word is a performative word: God acts by speaking, so that the liturgy is a divine drama. Yet the liturgy, as "the work of the people" (*leitourgia*), is simultaneously constituted by human acts and human speech. "God speaks by man," says von Balthasar,[11] and as Oswald Bayer remarks, "human speech is permeated with physicality. . . . Word and body, word and action are so bound up together that they cannot be separated."[12] It was with this two-fold human and divine character of the liturgy in mind that Martin Luther coined the phrase "the bodily word of the Gospel" (*das Leiblich Wort des Evangelii*), later taken up by Philip Melanchthon for inclusion in Article 5 of the German text of the *Augsburg Confession* (1530). By it Luther meant to indicate the whole verbal, ritual, and sacramental dynamic of the divine liturgy, in and through which Jesus Christ, God incarnate, personally communicates himself. The liturgy, in as much as it is a faithful and authentic proclamation of God's word, constitutes the tangible clothing in which Christ the Lord is to be encountered. It is noteworthy that the Reformer developed the use of this term "bodily" as a synonym of the term "external" in his polemical contests with the gnosticizing, anti-sacramental

---

9 Henri Bourgeois, "La Foi naît dans le corps," *La Maison-Dieu* 146 (1981), 40.

10 *Sacrosanctum concilium* (1963) §24.

11 Balthasar, "God has Spoken in Human Language," in *The Liturgy and the Word of God*, 33–52, at 46.

12 Oswald Bayer, *Living by Faith: Justification and Sanctification*, trans. Geoffrey W. Bromiley (Grand Rapids: Eerdmans, 2003), 47.

spiritualists from the mid-1520s onwards. In contrast to the Luther of the earlier tracts of 1520, we find here a thorough-going sacramentalist who grasps the constitutively physical character of divine-human union, one who would readily have affirmed Prétot's assertion that it is "by means of his body that man submits to the truth of his being 'before God.'"[13] For all the controversy subsequently attached to the so-called Reformation principle of *sola scriptura*, Luther rated the oral, aural, and public character of the divine word, that is, its mode as physical divine enactment, more highly than its written or "mental" form. Even if he did not entirely follow out the ecclesiological implications of this idea, he believed that it was through the human interpersonal communication that takes place physically in the enacted liturgy—with its verbal and sacramental proclamation of the gospel—that God most certainly engages and enters the human heart.[14]

Hearing and Faith

Of course Luther's sense of Scripture's essential and sacramental orality was not new. It is as old as desert monasticism, for which the Scriptures constituted "a speaking book."[15] Lively participation in the dramatic dialogue of the liturgy therefore calls for personal initiation into and increasing familiarity with the enscripturated story of salvation. While the liturgy as such is not primarily a didactic instrument, the public reading of holy Scripture, God's revealed and revealing word, possesses a certain pedagogical and formative function, calling for the incorporation of every human story into the definitive story of salvation.[16] The outward and public *lectio* both strengthens and is strengthened by

13 Patrick Prétot, "La Liturgie, Une Expérience Corporelle," *La Maison-Dieu* 247 (2006), 7–36, at 19.

14 See Bayer, *Living by Faith*, 47–49; also Adam G. Cooper, *Life in the Flesh: An Anti-Gnostic Spiritual Philosophy* (Oxford: Oxford University Press, 2008), 108–30.

15 William A. Graham, *Beyond the Written Word: Oral Aspects of Scripture in the History of Religion* (Cambridge: Cambridge University Press, 1993), 154.

16 See Rufus Black, *Christian Moral Realism: Natural Law, Narrative, Virtue, and the Gospel* (Oxford: Oxford University Press, 2000).

the life of inner and private *lectio*, the repetitive and attentive assimilation of the life-giving word of God. Here "prayer" and "meditation on the word" take place in one and the same activity. If psalmody is a response to the prevenient divine word, it is an assimilation of that word as well, for the psalms are both the word and the prayer of Christ, who continues to speak and pray in his members. This spiritual assimilation presumes a certain physical assimilation too, as the early tradition of *lectio divina* and the liturgy of the hours reveal. The Hebrew verb "to meditate" (*hagah*) means to ruminate on God's word, to chew it over, to murmur it out aloud again and again, like a lion growling over its prey (Ps. 1:2; 143:5; cf. Is. 31:4). Studies on the primitive Church's practice of prayer similarly disclose the overt physicality of the discipline, which lived on in the hesychastic tradition revived by Gregory Palamas in the fourteenth century.[17] The monks "would softly whisper the sacred words on their lips in order to imprint them not only on their mind but also on their body."[18] "Like a bee, [the monk] rummaged through the psalms incessantly, whispering to himself."[19] Reading aloud in this way multiplied the sensible modalities by which one could encounter Christ: not just through the eye, but through the ear and mouth as well. It thereby led to "a special kind of memorization,"[20] a recollection akin to *anamnesis* in which the reader imaginatively entered into the very world of the Scriptures, inserting himself into every detail of its dramatic, redemptive events. The Scriptures were thus able to penetrate more deeply into the reader's psychophysical universe, so that the central content of the Scriptures, Christ and his paschal mystery, increasingly determined his overall moral and spiritual vision.

We have been speaking of the way the primitive practitioners of *lectio divina*, even in their private contemplation, nonetheless

---

17 See Graham, *Beyond the Written Word*, 117–54; Douglas Burton-Christie, *The Word in the Desert: Scripture and the Quest for Holiness in Early Christian Monasticism* (Oxford: Oxford University Press, 1993); Mariano Margrassi, *Praying the Bible: An Introduction to Lectio Divina*, trans. Edward Hagman (Collegeville, Minnesota: Liturgical Press, 1998).

18 Margrassi, *Praying the Bible*, 66.

19 Ibid., 67.

20 Ibid., 92 n.106.

knew it as a verbal and physical exercise by which they deepened their affective and personal engagement with the word, so that in the end even the act of breathing became an essential component of "ceaseless prayer." In a similar way, for the encounter with the divine word to deepen its "bodily" and personal aspect, the private reading and contemplation of Scripture must lead and give way to its public reading and hearing.

How can we justify this assertion? There are two related aspects for consideration here. The first is the difference between reading and hearing. The second is the difference between the individual and the community. One must be careful not to pose any opposition between private and communal prayer. Yet the public divine service seems more manifestly to exhibit and preserve the proper relation between divine word (*Wort*) and personal response (*Antwort*), which in the eucharist are one. In the divine service, as always, the divine word is addressed not to the intellect, but to the whole person, who is always a bodily person in a communion of persons. The divine service teaches us first that faith is "born in the body," to borrow the phrase of Henri Bourgeois:

> To be sure, it is born in the heart, as biblical language has it. But even more it is constituted in the body. God is the God of bodies. . . . It is to bodies that he gives his Spirit and communicates the power of resurrection.[21]

Yet if we want to be even more specific, faith is conceived not just in the body in general, nor primarily through the eye, the classically accepted "organ" of intellectual insight, but through the ear, though which the word enters both the individual and communal body. Here again, Luther's emphasis upon hearing and the ear as the organ of faith was long preceded by the common medieval motif, arising in the fourth century, and later preserved only in the Latin Occident, known as *conceptio per aurem*.[22] The phrase

---

21 Bourgeois, "La Foi naît dans le corps," 41.

22 I have discussed this motif in greater detail in my article "Faith comes by hearing: a Pauline motif in theological tradition," *Lutheran Theological Journal* 44/2 (2010), 104–14.

refers to the understanding that Christ's conception took place by the seed of the word of God, spoken by the heavenly messenger, verbally entering Mary's ear.[23] Saint Augustine already knew of this motif: *Deus per angelum loquebatur et Virgo per aurem impregnebatur.*[24] The Syriac father, Ephraim the Syrus, contrasts it to the false hearing of Eve:

> In the beginning the serpent, getting possession of the ears of Eve, thence spread his poison throughout her whole body; today Mary through her ears received the champion of everlasting bliss.[25]

None of this is to deny that faith is of course a kind of seeing: "the light of faith makes us see what we believe."[26] Yet, as the biblical emphasis upon verbal theophany suggests, it is a vision that arises from hearing. Which is why Guardini asserts:

> The sacred word must be *heard*, not read. It should reach us through the ear, not through the eye. . . . The word that is written and read silently is different from the fresh, full word of sound. . . . [T]he word of mouth is always more powerful than the word of ink.[27]

Reading words on a page, I can avoid personal encounter. Listening to someone address me, I cannot.[28]

This concern for the intelligent and attentive reception of God's word, proclaimed in the liturgy in the form of an interpersonal dialogue, has been reiterated by thinkers as diverse as

---

23 See Nicholas P. Constas, "The *Conceptio per aurem* in Late Antiquity: Observations on Eve, the Serpent, and Mary," unpublished paper presented at the annual meeting of the North American Patristics Society (May, 1996); also Leo Steinberg, "How Shall This Be? Reflections on Filippo Lippi's 'Annunciation' in London, Part I," *Artibus et Historiae* 8/16 (1987), 25–44.

24 Quoted in Steinberg, "How Shall This Be?", 27.

25 Ibid.

26 ST II–II, 1, 4, ad 3.

27 Guardini, *Preparing Yourself for Mass*, 75–7.

28 "Listening is an interpersonal act; it involves two or more people in fairly close proximity. Reading involves one person with a book written by someone who can be miles away or centuries dead, or both. The listener is required to be attentive to the speaker and is more or less at the speaker's

Luther and Aquinas, for whom St. Paul's phrase "faith comes by hearing" (Rom. 10:17) has decisive import. Here we are thinking for example not only of Luther's preference for the *viva vox* over the written word, but of both his and Aquinas's belief that the sense of hearing is the privileged sensory mode by which supernatural faith is infused or engendered in the human heart. It is of the nature of faith to be related to a word, which in the case of God's word is not just a signifying sound but both a person and a promise embodying all that it signifies. Normally speaking, says Aquinas, "sight is more certain than hearing." (You hear an unrecognizable sound in the night, but only after turning on the light do you see and realize it is only the cat.) But since the objects of Christian faith are proposed by divine authority, "much more is a man certain about what he hears from God, who cannot be deceived, than about what he sees with his own reason, which can be mistaken."[29] Since the objects of faith are invisible and otherwise unknowable, they need to be believed on God's say-so.[30] Even in the eucharist, that most visible and tangible representation of divine realities, "hearing alone" is infallible:

> Visus, tactus, gustus, in te fallitur,
> Sed auditu solo tuto creditur:
> Credo quidquid dixit Dei filius
> Nihil veritatis verbo verius.

> Seeing, touching, tasting are in thee deceived;
> How says trusty hearing? That shall be believed;
> What God's Son has told me, take for truth I do;
> Truth himself speaks truly or there's nothing true.[31]

---

mercy. For the reader it is quite different, since the book is at the reader's mercy. . . . I can read by myself; I cannot listen by myself. In listening the speaker is in charge; in reading the reader is in charge." Eugene Peterson, *Working the Angles: The Shape of Pastoral Integrity* (Grand Rapids: Eerdmans, 1987), 62.

29 ST II–II, 4, 8 ad 2.

30 Ibid., 1, 4 ad 2.

31 From the famous eucharistic hymn ascribed to Aquinas, here rendered by Gerard Manley Hopkins.

Faith in the bare word of God, such as this, receiving its life through the senses, is indeed a real form of knowledge, but it is an inchoate knowledge. Until such time as it finally passes to the full knowledge of intelligent sight (1 Cor. 13:12), it remains appropriate to pray in the phrase proposed by Johann Georg Hamann: "Speak that I may see you."[32]

The Spirit in Prayer

According to the Johannine christological vision, one of the signs that the body of Jesus had become the new and definitive locus of divine-human communion was manifested at Jesus' baptism in the Jordan when the Holy Spirit was seen to descend and "remain" on him (Jn. 1:32–33). Then right towards the end of the Gospel, at the Johannine "Pentecost" on the eve of the first day of resurrection, Jesus breathes the same Holy Spirit upon his gathered Apostles (Jn. 20:22), sending them out with the indwelling Spirit "just as" he, the Son, had been sent from the Father. The parallels in these two events suggest a common purpose, as though "the sending of the Word of God (the Son) and the imparting of the Holy Spirit are but two phases of a single happening, in which divine life and truth are brought to man."[33] Could we not in turn suggest the existence of an ecclesial corollary to this mystery? David Bird identifies the Holy Spirit as "the living memory" or *anamnesis* of the Church, the one who brings alive and makes effective "in the present the wonderful deeds of God from the past."[34] Something similar was discerned by St. Irenaeus when he declared: "Where the Church is, there is the Spirit of God; and where the Spirit of God is, there is the Church, and every kind of grace."[35]

These words are directly pertinent to my discussion. Indeed, Hans Urs von Balthasar, in the source I have just quoted, draws

---

32 From Hamann's *Aesthetica in Nuce* (1762), in Kenneth Haynes (ed.), *Hamann: Writings on Philosophy and Language* (Cambridge: Cambridge University Press, 2007), 65.

33 Hans Urs von Balthasar, *Prayer*, trans. A. V. Littledale (London: SPCK, 1961), 55.

34 David Bird, *Heaven Revealed: The Holy Spirit and the Mass*, 32.

35 Irenaeus, *Against Heresies* 3, 24, 1.

upon the later patristic notion of *perichoresis* or *circumincessio* (mutual interpenetration) to describe the fundamentally trinitarian character and goal of Christian prayer, and thus the inseparability of the Word and the Spirit in every dimension of the Church's life, including the liturgical and bodily. "Christ's gift of his bodily and spiritual life to his own, reveals the incarnational aspect of the communication of the Spirit: we enter into the inner being of God through the wounded side of the Father's Son and Word."[36] Christ's death alone "can teach us that the Spirit of God is the Spirit of love; there we are shown the extreme of self-giving, and there the Son proves his love in the outpouring of his blood, the immolation of his flesh."[37] Following the Son's ascension to the Father, "the Son's glorified humanity participates in the eternal 'expiration' of the Holy Spirit, and the fruit of that outpouring of the Spirit is Christ's mystical body on earth."[38]

With this reference to the eternal, *ad intra* shape of the Spirit's relation to the Father through the Son, von Balthasar seeks to articulate an unchanging law by which the filiation of the Word in the sphere of creation, the sphere *ad extra*, also only occurs through the agency of the Spirit. Only the Spirit can disclose the inner mind of God to man (1 Cor. 2:12–16) and thereby incorporate man into the life and communion of God. He continues:

> For every real encounter with the Word presupposes a whole-hearted assent and acceptance on the part of man, and the assent on the part of Mary became, through her initial state of harmony with the Spirit and his descent on her, the source of the Incarnation of the Word. It was in the Spirit that she uttered her consent, an utterance that is the source of all Christian contemplation; it made her pregnant with the Word, made her treasure up all the words and ponder them in her heart.[39]

The tradition that held Mary to have conceived through hearing

36 Balthasar, *Prayer*, 56.
37 Ibid.
38 Ibid., 57.
39 Ibid., 58.

the word is the same tradition that holds her to be the archetype of the praying Church, since she is both Mother of God and daughter and bride of her Son. The entry of the word and the overshadowing of the Spirit coincide and interpenetrate in her, bringing about a double conception: in the flesh and in the Spirit. In Mary, as also in the Church, it is impossible to separate the gestation and contemplation of the word, the one in her body, the other in her heart. "The feminine, marial element in faith is a complete openness and readiness for the 'divine seed' that is to come, and it is also the contemplative element implanted deeply by the Holy Spirit in every act of faith."[40]

Experience tells us however that this is not how it always unfolds in the liturgies celebrated by the Christian faithful. In the Gospels Christ announces his teaching in public for all to hear. Yet he explains it to only a few, and even then the "inner hearing" does not always correspond to the "outer" hearing.[41] Hearing and understanding denote two dimensions that are properly but not always existentially connected. By "understanding" we do not mean the full grasp of reality realized in direct knowledge; not only do the divine mysteries lie beyond such a grasp, but it is the Spirit's special mission to help us in our weakness, to pray precisely when "we do not know how we ought to pray" (Rom. 8:27). Rather we mean to indicate all that arises from the first stirrings of faith, by which the outer voice of prayer utters: "Abba, Father!" (Rom. 8:15). This Spirit-inspired, filial address is the mark of authentic prayer. "Whatever depths be reached by human contemplation, if they are not, explicitly or implicitly, bound up with the life of the Trinity, the God-man and the Church, they are either illusory altogether or diabolic."[42] This comment would suggest that the faith-filled "understanding" subsequent to hearing is never attained in solitude, but presupposes the mediation of the Church and its magisterium, which in Peter and the Apostles has received from Christ the guarantee of indefectibility through the Spirit of truth (Mt. 16:17–18; Lk. 22:32; Jn. 16:12–15). Von Balthasar refers to this guarantee as "a nup-

---

40 Ibid.
41 See, for example, Mt. 13:1–17; 13:31–43.
42 Balthasar, *Prayer*, 61.

tial gift of the Incarnation," the assurance of the Church's "eternal, unfailing fidelity," on account of which "she is a mediator enabling the individual, who has no such assurance, to hear rightly."[43] The manner in which this guarantee is realized, which consists not only in official papal, episcopal, and conciliar formulations, but also—and perhaps most concretely and dynamically—in the actual exercise of the teaching office in the public liturgy, ensures that the understanding which constitutes the Church's living prayer remains a fully social reality, "and so the word of God, when it comes to the isolated person praying as part of the Church, comes attended, as it were, with an innumerable host of others praying with him."[44] Within the bosom of this social matrix alone is a person's nuptial relation with Christ preserved in its integrity, for the Church "has to correspond with her bridegroom, and she is enabled to do so in virtue of the word spoken to her."[45]

All this helps us to appreciate why the prayer of the Church is inseparable from the word of God proclaimed to, in, and by her. When she speaks, whether to God or to man, the Spirit speaks with her and in her. When she prays, she prays "in the name of Jesus," confidently approaching the Father "through him, with him, in him, in the unity of the Holy Spirit." And so her prayer is the performative speech-act of God no less than her proclamation, possessed as it is of a dogmatic normativity proper to its *"lex orandi"* character, as once proposed by Prosper of Aquitaine, and of an efficacy proper to a binding legal testimony, as once proposed by Jesus: "if two of you on earth agree about anything you ask for, it will be done for you by my Father in heaven" (Mt. 18:19). In sum, the performative efficacy of Christian prayer "extends as far as the effectiveness of the creative Word; better, it is itself that Word, it continues creation, it carries out the redemption of the world."[46]

43 Ibid., 69.

44 Ibid.

45 Ibid., 74.

46 Divo Barsotti, *La Parole de Dieu dans le mystère chrétien* (Paris: Cerf, 1954), 348; quoted by Joseph Gelineau, "The Church Responds to God with the Word of God," in *The Liturgy and the Word of God*, 84–98, at 90.

6

Sacrament and Sacrifice

IN THIS CHAPTER I arrive at the source and summit of my proposed liturgical theology of the body. The eucharistic celebration in the divine service represents the nuptial, covenantal event *par excellence*. It qualifies all the rest of the Church's liturgical activity, both individual and communal. By it the Church's spousality is activated and realized through her one-flesh incorporation into the new covenant established in Christ's death. My discussion is inspired in the main by the long and venerable tradition that reveres the wounded side of Christ's dead body as the birthplace of the Church, which the Fathers related to the sleep of Adam and the generation of Eve.[1] What is unique in the case of Christ, however, is that he was dead, not asleep. His fruitfulness as Messiah-husband, his power as paternal divine seed to generate life and impart the Spirit, is related immediately to his death, understood as his identification with the world's sin and climax of his humble obedience. It is likewise with the Church. Her fruitfulness, her capacity as spouse also to be mother, is tied to her experience of "a sacrificial lesion" or what tradition has called the "liquefaction" of ecstasis or the wounding of love by which, with the Apostle to the Gentiles, she fills up in her flesh what is still lacking with regard to Christ's sufferings (Col. 1:24).[2]

---

1 See Marc Cardinal Oullet, *Divine Likeness: Toward a Trinitarian Anthropology of the Family,* trans. Philip Milligan and Linda M. Cicone (Grand Rapids, Michigan: Eerdmans, 2006), 157–65.

2 McAleer, *Ecstatic Morality and Sexual Politics,* 82. See also Pierre Rousselot, "The 'Ecstatic' Conception of Love," in *id., The Problem of Love in the Middle Ages: A Historical Contribution,* trans. Alan Vincelette (Marquette University Press, 2001 [orig. 1908]), 152–211.

With these two related aspects in view, and recalling my over-all interest in the performative character of the liturgy, my primary questions will be to ask what shape the death of Christ takes in the ecclesial body, and in what sense the eucharist is simultaneously a sacrificial death, a marriage, and a fecund, life-giving ecstasis.

The Wounding of Christ

From the outset it seems necessary to start with the dogmatic affirmation that the eucharist is in fact some kind of sacrifice. In his 1980 Holy Thursday letter to Bishops on the Lord's Supper, John Paul II expressly identified the eucharist "above all else" as a sacrifice.[3] It is a "true" and "holy" sacrifice, a "consecrated offering," imparting to the Mass "sacrificial value" as the event which makes present "the sacrifice of our salvation," "the bloody propitiatory sacrifice" offered to the Father by Christ on the cross. Its sacrificial character derives in the first instance from Christ's unique sacrifice on the cross. "Indeed, he alone, giving himself as a propitiatory victim in an act of supreme surrender and immolation, has reconciled humanity with the Father, solely through his sacrifice. . . ."[4]

These comments suggest that to understand the eucharist as a sacrifice, we must first understand in what way Christ's death was a sacrifice. Here we cannot start from a general theory of sacrifice derived from a study of the history of religions, and from there try to impose a pattern upon the New Testament and the traditional liturgical sources. Rather we must begin with that particular, voluntary act of Jesus by which, in biblical language, he offered himself in death "as a ransom" for man (Mk. 10:45), and as "as a fragrant offering and sacrifice" to God (Eph. 5:2), thereby constituting himself as the universally valid *hilasterion*—the seat of appeal for divine mercy (Rom. 3:25; 1 Jn. 2:2). To be sure, this language of sacrifice and atonement carries an offensive ring today, allegedly insinuating "that God is appeased by cruelty

3 John Paul II, *Dominicae cenae* (1980) §9.
4 Ibid.

and wants nothing more than our obedience."[5] But any attempt
to efface it would negatively implicate the biblical and early
Christian witness, which from the most primitive times has interpreted Jesus' death in light of his own words, especially those spoken on the night of his betrayal, which themselves have roots in
the servant song of Isaiah, Israel's Passover liturgy, and covenantal sacrificial terminology (Is. 53:4–6; Ex. 12:12–23; Ex. 24:6–8; Jer.
31:31–34).[6] In that paschal meal, Jesus identifies himself, and particularly his body, as the sacrificial victim, the means of atonement, the unblemished offering which reconciles man to God. In
that intimate communion with his disciples he anticipates his
death as an act of divine love, a giving over of his body and life-
blood "for you and for many, for the forgiveness of sins." Time
and again the New Testament writers locate God's great reconciling act in "the blood of Christ's cross" and in "the body of his
flesh" given in death (Col. 1:20, 22). Universal redemption is
bought with "the precious blood of Christ, a lamb without blemish or defect" (1 Pet. 1:19). As high priest of a new covenant, Jesus
offers to God not "gifts and sacrifices" in the form of animal bodies, but his own body, willingly received as a gift, and willingly
given away. "And by that will," concludes the writer to the
Hebrews, that is, by the supreme freedom by which Christ consummated his life as a gift-for-others, "we have been made holy
through the sacrifice of the body of Jesus Christ, once for all"
(Heb. 10:5–10). Christ's sacrifice is not just a mental attitude or
rationally impartial decision on his part, but passionately involves
his whole body which in death becomes his oblation to the
Father and instrument of the world's sanctification. Without the
bodily aspect of this sacrificial gift, which in Christ's case involved
surrender to an ignominious physical death, there can be no

5 Rita Brock and Rebecca Parker, *Proverbs of Ashes: Violence, Redemption and
the Search for What Saves Us* (Boston: Beacon Press, 2001), 30. For a contrary
view, see John Dunnill, "Communicative Bodies and Economies of Grace: The
Role of Sacrifice in the Christian Understanding of the Body," *Journal of Religion* 83/1 (2003), 79–94.

6 See further Robert J. Daly, *The Origins of the Christian Doctrine of Sacrifice*
(London: Darton, Longman and Todd, 1978); Joachim Jeremias, *The Eucharistic
Words of Jesus*, trans. Norman Perrin (London: SCM, 1966).

Church, which is born from the outflow of his blood and water and the *transitus* of his Spirit (Jn. 19:30). As McAleer puts it, "it is this liquefaction of Jesus's body that is the anterior condition of the Eucharist, and the community founded therein."[7]

Considered as an act of total self-entrustment to the Father, a decision engaging his whole being, Christ's wounding and sacrifice on the cross can be understood as the supreme act of human freedom.[8] Yet it is vital to perceive that this human act itself springs from the heart of divine love. His sacrifice is simultaneously a sacrament, the absolutely unexpected, gratuitous, and performative movement of God toward a "lost" and "powerless" creation (Lk. 19:10; Rom. 5:6–8). Wanting to define divine love, St. John could point to the cross-event and say: "this is love" (1 Jn. 4:10). For St. Paul, this cross with its subversive rationale (*logos*) is salvific power (Rom. 1:16). Joseph Ratzinger's comments fittingly summarize my point:

> The initiative in the sacrifice of Jesus Christ comes from God. . . . Christ is not in the first instance a gift *we* men bring to an angry God; rather, the fact that he is there at all, living, suffering, loving, is the work of God's love.[9]

The Wounding of the Church

Even if, in contrast to the more materialistic practices of pagan and Jewish worship, primitive Christianity tended to spiritualize the idea of sacrifice, and even if, inspired by Jesus' own words, it understood the phrase "taking up one's cross" in terms of a particular mode of conduct (cf. Mt. 10:38; 16:24), it will not do to reduce Christian sacrifice to a purely ethical, non-cultic notion.[10] Not, at least, if the New Testament passages I have cited above are to have any meaning. Notwithstanding the surge of interest

---

7 McAleer, *Ecstatic* Morality, 76.

8 See John Paul II, *Fides et ratio* (1998) §13.

9 Joseph Ratzinger, *God is Near Us: The Eucharist, Heart of Life*, trans. Henry Taylor (San Francisco: Ignatius, 2003), 45.

10 *Pace* Daly, *The Origins of the Christian Doctrine of Sacrifice*, 140.

from the eleventh to the sixteenth centuries in determining with precision such details as the agent, moment and modality of sacrificial immolation in the Mass, along with certain emphases evident in the Tridentine reforms, which, sensitive to the Protestant situation, aimed partly at shoring up the sacrificial character of the Mass, the Church has never really lost sight of the twofold character of the eucharist as both sacrifice and sacrament. In his *Corpus Mysticum*, Henri de Lubac amassed a vast array of sources from the first millenium in which, almost universally, sacrament and sacrifice are regarded as indivisibly and reciprocally united. The action that takes place in the eucharist is "a ritual echo, endlessly reverberating in time and space, of the unique action from which it takes its sense."[11] At the same time, "[t]he external sacrifice and ritual is also the sacrament of the 'true' sacrifice, of that interior and spiritual sacrifice by which the holy society of all those who belong to God is brought into being." In a passage from Augustine often quoted by Aquinas, "Every work we perform in order to cleave to God in holy fellowship is a true sacrifice. . . . A visible sacrifice is the sacrament of an invisible sacrifice."[12] Sacrifice, if it has any relation to sacrament, that is, if it is understood christologically in the way I have already delineated, is at once ethical and cultic. It is both gift received and gift offered and lived.

Having said that, and without in any way detracting from or calling into question the fact of the real presence, it is quite possible to distinguish between the sacrifice performed by Christ on the cross and the sacrifice which recurs in the Mass, which is the sacrifice offered by the whole Church in and with her priests. The great liturgiologist Joseph Jungmann stressed that the structure of the Mass, from beginning to end, "portrays it as *our sacrifice*; it is our entering into the sacrifice of Christ, it is our affiliation with his oblation to the heavenly Father—so much so, that the symbols of his oblation, the offerings of his body and blood, are

---

11 Henri de Lubac, *Corpus Mysticum: The Eucharist and the Church in the Middle Ages*, trans. Gemma Simmonds *et al.* (Notre Dame, Indiana: University of Notre Dame Press, 2006), 62.

12 Augustine, *City of God* 10, 6. See Aquinas ST II–II, 81, 7; II–II, 85, 2.

allowed to represent our offering also."[13] This conclusion seems to be supported by an important line of evidence in the tradition. According to de Lubac, it was the one of the functions of the word "mystical" to distinguish the "body of Christ" in the sacrament from, and relate it to, the celestial body of Christ once offered on the cross and the ecclesial body of Christ which is the Church.[14] What this seems to suggest is that even though the primary action in the eucharist is Christ's, and the primary movement from God toward man, the Church here is not dispossessed of her own subjectivity. She too sacrifices here. Her sacrifice is of course a "sacrifice of thanksgiving," a response, the priestly service of God consisting in the fruit of lips that praise and confess his name (Heb. 13:15; 1 Pet. 2:9). It is the "living sacrifice" of bodies made holy by baptism and the concomitant renewal of the mind (Rom. 12:1). But it is also the sacrifice of a "broken spirit" and "contrite heart" (Ps. 51:17), sacrificial offerings which suggest a real connaturality between the worshipping Church and "the man of sorrows," the humble Messiah "familiar with suffering" (Is. 53:3). Von Hildebrand has identified this humble, reverent spirit before the all-holy Trinity as the chief mark of the Church in the eucharistic anaphora:

> The holy Sacrifice of the Mass is especially penetrated with this Spirit: the necessity of sacrificing to God, the impossibility of offering him an adequate sacrifice because of our poverty, the sacrificial prayer of Christ in which we are allowed to participate, the primal, classical attitude before God, the "Per ipsum, cum ipso, et ipso est tibi, Deo Patri omnipotenti, in unitate Spiritus Sancti, omnis honor et gloria. . . ."[15]

Ratzinger also has commented upon this humble character of the Church's subjectivity in the eucharistic prayer, which in turn derives from Christ's own self-emptying humility. The celebrant

---

13 Joseph Jungmann, *Announcing the Word of God*, trans. Ronald Walls (London: Burns and Oates, 1967), 14.

14 De Lubac, *Corpus Mysticum*, 73.

15 Dietrich von Hildebrand, *Liturgy and Personality* (Baltimore: Helicon Press, 1960), 42.

does not act in his own name, but in the name of the Church whose sacrifice it is, even if it is offered "at his hands" ("May the Lord accept this sacrifice at your hands. . . ."). But these words do not yet convey the total picture. In praying the eucharistic prayer the priest acts in the name of the Church. But at the same time he acts *in persona Christi*, a fact most poignantly revealed when he speaks in the first person in the words of consecration, *"Hoc est corpus meum."* It is Christ himself who speaks these words, and so it is Christ himself who offers this sacrifice, concorporately including the body of his Church within himself in making it a sacrament of salvation, a nuptial performance of fruitful divine love. Yet even in this sacrifice which the Church offers in, with, and through Christ, she is no passive spectator. In the words of Marc Ouellet, "Eucharistic communion is not unilateral."[16] On the contrary:

> The magnitude of Christ's achievement consists precisely in his not remaining someone else, over and against us, who might thus relegate us once more to a merely passive role; he does not merely bear with us; rather, he bears us up; he identifies himself with us to such an extent that our sins belong to him and his being to us: *he truly accepts us and takes us up, so that we ourselves become active with his support and alongside him, so that we ourselves cooperate and join in the sacrifice with him, participating in the mystery ourselves.*[17]

It is precisely through this physical, sacramental sharing in the filial humility of the Son who, in his sacrificial self-oblation, "poured out his life unto death" (Is. 53:12), that the praying Church becomes herself, participating in and experiencing for herself, as the very condition of her being, the cruciform liquefaction of Christ's body and the fecund wounding of his divine love, offered to the Father for the salvation of the world. This wounding is liturgically manifest in the deposition of self both presupposed and enacted in the Church's humble offering of gifts, her response to the *sursum corda*, her anaphoral and epicletic prayer with

16 Ouellet, *Divine Likeness*, 156.
17 Ratzinger, *God is Near Us*, 50.

Christ, her kiss of peace received and bestowed, and her subsequent somatic union in one loaf and one cup. The convergence of sacrament and sacrifice in the eucharist in this way again assumes an intensely nuptial character:

> To receive into me the One who was sacrificed for me means to grant him space in, and power of disposition over, my whole existence, both spiritual and physical, and thereby to follow him—at a distance, since it is he (in a masculine fashion) who decides, whilst I (in a feminine fashion) let him act, but also in unity, since, through my letting him act, he will decide in me only in accordance with the meaning of his own *disponibilité*. And so the meal becomes the Church's real sharing in Jesus' flesh and blood in their condition of victimhood. . . .[18]

And all of this is justly called "worship," "thanksgiving," "sacrifice." Without this at-once ethical and cultic dimension to her sacrificial vocation, the Church's faith would become fruitless, loveless, and unformed. Without it, she would cease to be herself.

Death and Resurrection

"As the verse of the *Ave Verum* reminds us, Catholic *traditio*, by referring baptism and the Eucharist to the pierced side of the Crucified One, has always strongly emphasized the direct relationship between Jesus Christ and sacramental action."[19] Like baptism, the eucharist gives life paradoxically by uniting to Christ's death. Like baptism, the eucharist bodily realizes a new covenantal relationship. These two sacramental ideas—death and covenant—are theologically and liturgically related. According to the New Testament writer to the Hebrews, a covenant (*diatheke*) only comes into effect when the person who made it dies (Heb. 9:16–17). In the liturgy, the repeated *anamnesis* of the institutional event, the

---

18 Hans Urs von Balthasar, *Mysterium Paschale: The Mystery of Easter*, trans. Aidan Nichols (San Francisco: Ignatius, 2000), 99.

19 Angelo Cardinal Scola, *The Nuptial Mystery*, trans. Michelle K. Borras (Grand Rapids, Michigan: Eerdmans, 2005), 296.

repeated acclamation of the "lamb of God who takes away the sin of the world," the repeated use of Christ's justifying blood (Rom. 5:9), without the shedding of which "there can be no forgiveness" (Heb. 9:22): all bring about a proclamation of his death as womb of the church's eschatological life, of his wounding as the nuptial consummation of God's ultimate covenant with man. But do these specific references from Hebrews deal with the new covenant or the old, and what role do they accord to Christ's resurrected and glorified body which, mystically made available for consumption in the eucharist, is regarded by the Fathers of the Church as the pledge and guarantee of our deification?

To answer these questions, the passages quoted from the letter to the Hebrews call for closer analysis. In this section the new covenant is contrasted with the old, which came into effect when Moses took the blood of calves and applied it to the people (Heb. 9:18–20; cf. Ex. 24:4–8). Such a covenant, however, could never of itself bestow true forgiveness, "because it is impossible for the blood of bulls and goats to take away sins" (Heb. 10:4). This then raises the question as to the meaning of the sentence, "without the shedding of blood there is no forgiveness" (Heb. 9:22). Does it refer to what happened under the old covenant with Moses? Or does it refer to what happens in the new covenant with Christ? If it refers to what happened with Moses, why is it in the present tense, and why does it connect forgiveness with the shedding of blood, if the blood of animals was powerless to effect forgiveness? Because this is such an important question, and relates directly to the new covenant instituted in the Lord's Supper, it seems appropriate to examine this sentence further.

The Greek word usually translated as "the shedding of blood" is *haimatekchysia*, a compound made up from the words *haima* (blood) and *ekchein* (to pour out or splash). In its verb form it can mean two things. First, it can mean "to kill" or "to take someone's life," as we find in the Greek Old Testament in Genesis 9:6: "Whoever *sheds the blood* of man, by man shall his *blood be shed*." Secondly, it can mean "to pour out blood" or "to apply blood" in some kind of ceremony. An example of this meaning is found in Leviticus 4:7 (LXX): "The rest of the blood *he shall pour out* at the base of the altar."

Looking at the context of Hebrews 9:22, one could plausibly argue that the word *haimatekchysia* is being used in the first sense as referring to death or the taking of life. Just as a will comes into effect only at death, so the old "will" or testament (*diatheke*) came into effect only with the death of an appropriate sacrificial animal, a death proved or ratified by Moses' use of its blood (cf. Ex. 24:4–8). Such ratification of the covenant in turn points typologically to the new "will" or testament instituted by Jesus and brought into effect by his death.

However, given that Hebrews 9:22 speaks of forgiveness in the present tense, and that Hebrews 10:4 asserts that animal blood can never take away sins, it seems more appropriate to conclude that it is the second meaning of the word *haimatekchysia* that is chiefly in mind, namely, the *pouring out* or *application* of blood, and that not just of animal blood, but of Jesus' blood. Notice that in the immediately preceding verses (Heb. 9:19–21) it is not the *death* of the sacrificial victim that is emphasized but *what is done with its blood*. In this respect the sentence surely points to Christ—of course presupposing his death but especially directing us to his high priestly ministry, following his resurrection and ascension, in which he applies the saving fruits of his death. Just as Moses entered into the earthly tabernacle and "sprinkled" its furnishings with the blood of animals (Heb. 9:21), so now Christ, having offered his body in sacrifice once for all on the cross, and having been declared in exaltation by the Father to be Son and priest "forever" (Heb. 5:5–6), has entered the heavenly tabernacle with his own blood, where he pours it out or applies it to cleanse not external things but the very hearts and consciences of those who draw near in faith (Heb. 9:14). The words of institution seem to confirm that this ongoing priestly ministry of Christ in the heavenly sanctuary actually takes place in the eucharist by the use of a closely related word also meaning "to pour out" (*ekchynnein*): "This is my blood of the covenant which is being poured out for many for the forgiveness of sins" (Mt. 26:28).

This brief exegetical excursus has been included in order to strengthen the claim that the eucharist, not apart from its foundation in Christ's sacrificial death, is also the performative priestly and nuptial act of the risen Lord in which is anticipated and proleptically realized the eschatological marriage of the bride and the Lamb. It is only by participating in Christ's once crucified and now risen flesh that we are lifted up into the eternal, into the triune communion of persons. The mystery of faith proclaimed by the faithful in the eucharistic liturgy points three ways: back to Christ's death, here to his hidden presence, and forward to his glorious *parousia*. Those theologies that reduce the eucharist to a commemoration in the order of the first dimension only, or which focus exclusively upon the words of institution (with or without reference to possible Aramaic antecedents), or those which admit Christ's presence in the assembly but only in an ethereal, "spiritual" or generically "personal" form, seem equally to miss the full meaning and power of the eucharist as the risen Lord's enfleshed nuptial enactment, a real coming together of the celestial and ecclesial body of Christ, by means of the participated sacramental body, within the heart of the Trinity. Both the words of institution and Christ's death would have remained meaningless without the resurrection:

> whereby it is made clear that these words were spoken with divine authority, that his love is indeed strong enough to reach out beyond death. Thus the three belong together: the word, the death, and the Resurrection. And this trinity of word, death, and Resurrection, which gives us an inkling of the mystery of the triune God himself, this is what Christian tradition calls the 'Paschal Mystery,' the mystery of Easter. Only these three together make up a whole, only these three together constitute a veritable reality, and this single mystery of Easter is the source and origin of the Eucharist.[20]

In support of this claim, one could make recourse to the deep stream of patristic reflection on the soteriological instrumentality of Christ's crucified and risen flesh, which Cyril of Alexandria, for example, habitually referred to, with specific reference to the eucharist, as "life-giving" (*zoopoion*). The eucharist entails contact with this divine, life-giving flesh as well as encounter with the

---

20 Ratzinger, *God is Near Us*, 43–4.

word of Christ's almighty command.[21] But since we are nearing the end of our study, it will suffice to draw upon a little known strand in the tradition which focuses upon the correspondence between the eating commanded by Christ at the inauguration of the new covenant and the eating forbidden by God at the beginning of history. Both events revolve around eating, at once the most basic physical impulse and the highest form of societal bonding, and both bring about a new and different relation to death.[22] In an illuminating comment on this correspondence unearthed by de Lubac in his *Corpus Mysticum*, St. Thomas relates the two meals in terms of malady and cure, sin and satisfaction, food of death and food of life, hearing the devil and hearing the Saviour, sensual satiety and sensual poverty, revelation and concealment, unbelief and faith:

> A cure for infidelity requires that the body of Christ be veiled, so that to the fault of infidelity there should correspond a congruent mode of satisfaction. Consequently, as the unbelief of the first parents began with the hearing of the words of the devil recommending the food that had death concealed within it, and which their senses took intense delight, so it was fitting that the faith of those to be saved should begin from hearing the word of the Saviour, recommending a food that has true life hidden within it, and in which our senses are piously deceived.[23]

Inasmuch as the eucharist is food with "true life hidden within it," and inasmuch as the mortal bodies who eat the "veiled" body and blood of Christ, in contrast to the normal manner of assimilating other foods, are themselves assimilated to his immortal body, death is exposed in its verity as both "the last enemy" and the mode of fruitful nuptial union. Just as there can be no resurrection without death, so there can be no marriage without "the lesion of sacrifice." There is a curious paradox here, which seems

21 See Cooper, *Life in the Flesh*, 77–83.
22 See Bourgeois, 'La Foi naît dans le corps," 57–63.
23 *Opuscule* 51 and *De sacramento altaris* 7, quoted by Henri de Lubac, *Corpus Mysticum*, 334.

to go hand in hand with the paradox of bodily existence, which cannot be considered in its concrete reality apart from death. The Church speaks of an eternal heavenly marriage. What does this mean for us bodily, if we must die? "Taste and see," answers one who is both priest and victim.

> In all ages, and among all peoples, the ultimate aim of men in their festivals has been to open the door of death. . . . Death is the ultimate question, and wherever it is bracketed out there can be no real answer. Only when this question is answered can men truly celebrate and be free. The Christian feast, the Eucharist, plumbs the very depths of death.[24]

It is because the eucharist is the feast of Christ's cross, the feast of "the Lamb slain from the foundation of the world" (Rev. 13:8), that it is also the fountain and tree of life, whose leaves are "for the healing of the nations" (Rev. 22:2). The reversal of death through death, communicated bodily under the veil of the Church's own faith-filled self-oblation, spells the arrival of nuptial life, which is to say, the arrival of being itself.

24 Ratzinger, *God is Near Us*, 44.

Conclusion

The Prophetism of the Body

THIS BOOK BEGAN by outlining an understanding of theology as a liturgical and physical encounter. Calling this experience "liturgical theology," it raised the possibility of its conceptual application to the body as the latter has come to be understood in the personalistic and nuptial terms of John Paul II's theology of the body. It further suggested the need for an understanding of the liturgy as performative divine action, on the basis of which it is possible to speak of a prophetism of the liturgical body. This dual package, consisting in a liturgical theology of the body on the one hand and a performative understanding of liturgical action on the other, gives rise to the notion of a "performative nuptiality."

In chapter one, I proceeded to lay down a series of metaphysical principles as the necessary conceptual apparatus by which to undertake an analysis of the liturgy as performative nuptiality. Beginning with the revealed Christian doctrine of creation by divine love, these principles conceptualize being in terms of act, relation, and receptivity. Material being is inescapably erotic and ecstatic, and yet comes to its proper fulfilment not simply by its own actuation, but above all by suffering divine love.

In chapter two I applied this metaphysic, in a more focussed way, to concrete liturgical action. The nuptial drama, enacted in the liturgy as "theodrama," involves an interplay between activity and passivity, with God as the primary "actor." The performativity of the liturgy depends precisely on this personal involvement on God's part, and on the character of the incarnation as divine "speech-act," so that the liturgy realizes the extension of God's bodily economy. On this basis, I argued that the architectural and spatial dimensions of the ritual drama are by no means incidental to its purposeful realization.

Building upon the insights of chapters one and two, chapter three explored the role of sensible symbols and typology in the liturgy. Since the deployment of symbols is not simply a matter of external adornment, but actually constitutes the liturgy as performative theodrama, the scope of symbolic fluidity is constrained by limits stemming from the semitive character of certain stable, archetypal signs. Some symbols cannot be exchanged or replaced without detriment to their referential capacity, a fact with immediate import for the effective nuptial symbolism of the Church's worship.

From this point I proceeded in chapters four through six to analyze three primary pairings in which the metaphysical and liturgical principles enunciated in chapters one to three come to bear: 1) Christ and priest, 2) word and prayer, and 3) sacrifice and sacrament. The common focus in all three rests in the constitutive physicality of Christian worship, apart from which divine-human nuptiality remains an abstraction. However, it was also argued that it is not through physicality *per se*, but through a certain complementary, divinely instituted, sacramental order that the Word of God, ever incarnate, mystically and fruitfully betroths himself in covenantal grace to his church/spouse/bride. Yet this primacy of the Word does not rob the Church of her proper subjectivity. Indeed, it is as she sacramentally suffers the wounding liquefaction of Christ's sacrificial love that she participates in his sacrifice and so becomes the salvific agent she is called to be. In this sense the liturgy points three ways—back to Christ's self-gift in death, here and now to the hidden presence and spousal performance of that event, and forward to its perfect and manifest consummation in the eschatological marriage of the bride and the Lamb.

My closing comments follow on from this point. For it is here that we can again usefully speak of the prophetism of the (liturgical) body. Just as a theology of the body rests on the fact that the body, and only the body, is capable of making the invisible visible, so that the body may veritably be understood as a sacramental sign,[1] so the body which is the Church—and specifically the

1 TOB, 203.

Church at worship, the Church that becomes a concrete, subsisting subject in eucharistic communion—mystically manifests in time and space the invisible reality that is Jesus Christ the Word made flesh, who in his own person embodies and anticipates the spousal union of the Trinity and deified creation. But like the prophetism at work in the rite of holy matrimony, in which the couple exchange vows and announce in word and promise what is yet to take effect in deed and fulfilment, so the liturgy involves a certain yearning restraint, a certain "not-yet-ness" or "eschatological contradiction,"[2] recognizable in the contingent, promissory, repetitive and sacramental forms that characterize the liturgical celebration. If there is a possibility of falsification here, as there is in the case when a couple partially withhold in physical union all they have pledged in the marriage rite to give without reserve, it lies not on the side of the eschatological nuptial union of Christ and the Church, but within the enacted liturgy itself. It is there that the word of God and the semitive symbols can be falsified or misused. It is there that the individual participants in the drama can fall into distraction or infidelity. It is for this reason that the liturgy must be regarded not as a sum of parts, each consisting in this or that individual's personal faith or devotion, nor simply as a human response to a real but long-past event, but as a performative redemptive drama whose efficacy is finally guaranteed by the gratuitous, undeserved faithfulness of the divine lover. So it is that all analogies break down, even the analogy of human marriage, which in this life will never quite perfectly embody that "great mystery" whose glorious lineaments will only come to full light in the resurrection when the bride of Christ will no longer be veiled in humility but will appear in all her immaculate and radiant beauty.

2 See Chauvet, *Symbol and Sacrament*, 546.

Bibliography

Special Texts or Collections

Aquinas, Saint Thomas. *Summa Theologiae*. 61 vols. London: Blackfriars, 1964–80.

Carlem, Claudia, ed. *The Papal Encyclicals 1958–1981*. Ann Arbor: Prieran Press, 1990.

Kittel, Gerhard, and Gerhard Friedrich, eds. *Theological Dictionary of the New Testament*. Translated by Geofrey W. Bromiley, 10 vols. Grand Rapids: Eerdmans, 1964–74.

Papal and Conciliar documents: http://www.vatican.va/phome_en.htm

Tanner, Norman P. *Decrees of the Ecumenical Councils*. 2 vols. London: Sheed and Ward, 1990.

Primary Sources in Translation

Aquinas, Saint Thomas. *Truth*. vol 3. Translated by Robert W. Schmidt. Chicago: Henry Regnery, 1954.

———. *Thomas Aquinas: Selected Philosophical Writings*. Translated by Timothy McDermott. Oxford: Oxford University Press, 1993.

Augustine, Saint. *City of God*. Edited by David Knowles. Translated by Henry Bettenson. London: Penguin, 1972.

Clark, Mary T., ed. *An Aquinas Reader: Selections from the Writings of Thomas Aquinas*. London: Hodder and Stoughton, 1972.

Cooper, John M., ed. and trans. *Plato: Complete Works*. Cambridge: Hackett, 1997.

Evagrius Ponticus. *The Praktikos and Chapters on Prayer*. Translated by John Eudes Bamberger. Cistercian Studies Series 4. Kalamazoo, Michigan: Cistercian Publications, 1981.

Luibheid, Colm, trans. *Pseudo-Dionysius: The Complete Works*. The Classics of Western Spirituality. London: SPCK, 1987.

McCauley, Leo P., and Anthony A. Stephenson. *The Works of Cyril of Jerusalem*. Washington D.C.: Catholic University of America Press, 1970.

Origen. *An Exhortation to Martyrdom, Prayer, First Principles et al.* Translated by Rowan A. Greer. London: SPCK, 1979.

———. *The Song of Songs, Commentary and Homilies.* Ancient Christian Writers 26. Translated by R. P. Lawson. New York: Newman Press, 1957.

Ramsey, Boniface and John E. Rotelle, eds. *The Works of Saint Augustine: A Translation for the 21st Century.* 50 vols. New York: New City Press, 1990.

Roberts, Alexander, and James Donaldson, eds. *Ante-Nicene Fathers.* 10 vols. Peabody, Massachusetts: Hendrickson, 1995.

Schaff, Philip, ed. *Nicene and Post-Nicene Fathers Series 1.* 14 vols. Peabody, Massachusetts: Hendrickson, 1995.

———. *Nicene and Post-Nicene Fathers Series 2.* 14 vols. Peabody, Massachusetts: Hendrickson, 1995.

Yarnold, Edward, trans. *Cyril of Jerusalem.* The Early Church Fathers. London and New York: Routledge, 2000.

Other Works

Adam, Karl. *The Spirit of Catholicism.* Translated by Dom. Justin McCann. London: Sheed and Ward, 1929.

D'Andia, Ysabel, "Eros and Agape: The Divine Passion of Love." *Communio* 24 (1997): 29–50.

Balthasar, Hans Urs von. *Prayer.* Translated by A. V. Littledale. London: SPCK, 1961.

———. *Explorations in Theology II: The Spouse of the Word.* Translated by A. V. Littledale. San Francisco: Ignatius, 1991.

———. "Thoughts on the Priesthood of Women." *Communio* 23 (1996): 701–9.

———. *Theo-Drama: Theological Dramatic Theory, vol. 2: The Dramatis Personae: Man in God.* Translated by Graham Harrison. San Francisco: Ignatius, 1990 (orig. 1976).

———. *Theo-Drama: Theological Dramatic Theory, vol. 3: The Dramatis Personae: The Person in Christ.* Translated by Graham Harrison. San Francisco: Ignatius, 1992 (orig. 1978).

———. *Theo-Drama: Theological Dramatic Theory, vol. 5: The Last Act.* Translated by Graham Harrison. San Francisco: Ignatius, 1998 (orig. 1983).

———. *Mysterium Paschale: The Mystery of Easter.* Translated by Aidan Nichols. San Francisco: Ignatius, 2000 (orig. 1970).

———. *Cosmic Liturgy: The Universe According to Maximus the Confessor.* Translated by Brian E. Daley. San Francisco: Ignatius, 2003.

Bayer, Oswald. "Notae Ecclesiae." In *Lutheran Contributions to the Missio Dei.* Geneva: Lutheran World Federation, 1984.

———. *Promissio: Geschichte der reformatorischen Wende in Luthers Theologie.* 2nd ed. Darmstadt: Wissenschaftliche Buchgesellschaft, 1989.

———. *Living by Faith: Justification and Sanctification.* Translated by Geoffrey W. Bromiley. Grand Rapids, Michigan: Eerdmans, 2003.

Betz, Hans Dieter. *Galatians: A Commentary on Paul's Letter to the Churches in Galatia.* Philadelphia: Fortress, 1979.

Bird, David. *The Royal Road to Joy: The Beatitudes and the Eucharist.* Chicago: Hillenbrand, 2003.

———. *Heaven Revealed: The Holy Spirit and the Mass.* Leominster, Herefordshire: Gracewing, 2008.

Black, Rufus. *Christian Moral Realism: Natural Law, Narrative, Virtue, and the Gospel.* Oxford: Oxford University Press, 2000.

Bourgeois, Henri. "La Foi naît dans le corps." *La Maison-Dieu* 146 (1981), 39–67.

Brock, Rita and Rebecca Parker. *Proverbs of Ashes: Violence, Redemption and the Search for What Saves Us.* Boston: Beacon Press, 2001.

Burton-Christie, Douglas. *The Word in the Desert: Scripture and the Quest for Holiness in Early Christian Monasticism.* Oxford: Oxford University Press, 1993.

Butler, Sara. *The Catholic Priesthood and Women: A Guide to the Teaching of the Church.* Chicago: Hillenbrand Books, 2007.

Cavalletti, Sofia. *Living Liturgy: Elementary Reflections.* Chicago: Liturgy Training Publications, 1998.

Chauvet, Louis-Marie. *Symbol and Sacrament: A Sacramental Reinterpretation of Christian Existence.* Translated by Patrick Madigan and Madeleine Beaumont. Collegeville, Minnesota: Liturgical Press, 1995.

Clarke, W. Norris. *Person and Being.* Milwaukee: Marquette University Press, 1993.

Cochini, Christian. *The Apostolic Origins of Priestly Celibacy.* Translated by Nelly Marans. San Francisco: Ignatius, 1990.

Constas, Nicholas P. "The *Conceptio per aurem* in Late Antiquity: Observations on Eve, the Serpent, and Mary." Unpublished paper presented at the annual meeting of the North American Patristics Society, May 1996.

Cooper, Adam G. "Christ as Teacher of Theology: Praying the Our

Father with Origen and Maximus." In *Origeniana Octava: Origene e la Tradizione Alessandrina*, edited by Lorenzo Perrone. Leuven: Peters, 2003.

———. *The Body in Saint Maximus the Confessor: Holy Flesh, Wholly Deified*. Oxford: Oxford University Press, 2005.

———. *Life in the Flesh: An Anti-Gnostic Spiritual Philosophy*. Oxford: Oxford University Press, 2008.

Crammer, Corinne. "One sex or two? Balthasar's theology of the sexes." In *The Cambridge Companion to Hans Urs von Balthasar*, edited by Edward T. Oakes and David Moss. Cambridge: Cambridge University Press, 2004.

Daly, Robert J. *The Origins of the Christian Doctrine of Sacrifice*. London: Darton, Longman and Todd, 1978.

Daniélou, Jean. *The Bible and the Liturgy*. London: Darton, Longman and Todd, 1960.

Dodd, C.H. *The Fourth Gospel*. Cambridge: Cambridge University Press, 1958.

Dunnill, John. "Communicative Bodies and Economies of Grace: The Role of Sacrifice in the Christian Understanding of the Body." *Journal of Religion* 83/1 (2003), 79–94.

Fagerberg, David W. *What is Liturgical Theology? A Study in Methodology*. Collegeville, Minnesota: Liturgical Press, 1992.

Galot, Jean. *Theology of the Priesthood*. San Francisco: Ignatius, 1985.

Gamber, Klaus. *The Reform of the Roman Liturgy: Its Problems and Background*. Translated by Klaus D. Grimm. San Juan Capristrano, California: Una Voce Press, 1993.

Graham, William A. *Beyond the Written Word: Oral Aspects of Scripture in the History of Religion*. Cambridge: Cambridge University Press, 1993.

Guardini, Romano. *Preparing Yourself for Mass*. Manchester, NH: Sophia Institute Press, 1993 (orig. 1939).

Guindon, Andre. *The Sexual Language: An Essay in Moral Theology*. Ottawa: University of Ottawa Press, 1977.

Hauke, Manfred. *Women in the Priesthood? A Systematic Analysis in the Light of the Order of Creation and Redemption*. Translated by David Kipp. San Francisco: Ignatius, 1988.

Haynes, Kenneth, ed. *Hamann: Writings on Philosophy and Language*. Cambridge: Cambridge University Press, 2007.

Hayward, Robert. *The Jewish Temple: A Non-biblical Sourcebook*. London: Routledge, 1996.

Hildebrand, Dietrich von. *Liturgy and Personality*. Baltimore: Helicon Press, 1960.

Jeremias, Joachim. *The Eucharistic Words of Jesus*. Translated by Norman Perrin. London: SCM, 1966.

John Paul II, Pope. *Man and Woman He Created Them: A Theology of the Body*. Translated by Michael Waldstein. Boston: Pauline, 2006.

Jungmann, Joseph. *Announcing the Word of God*. Translated by Ronald Walls. London: Burns and Oates, 1967.

Kavanagh, Aidan. *On Liturgical Theology*. New York: Pueblo, 1984.

———. *Elements of Rite: A Handbook of Liturgical Style*. Collegeville, Minnesota: Liturgical Press, 1990.

Kleinig, John W. *Leviticus*. Saint Louis: Concordia, 2003.

le Fort, Gertrud von. *The Eternal Woman: The Timeless Meaning of the Feminine*. Translated by Marie Cecilia Buehrle. San Francisco: Ignatius, 2010.

Lewis, C. S. *Undeceptions: Essays on Theology and Ethics*. Edited by Walter Hooper. London: Geoffrey Bles, 1971.

Martimort, A. G., Pierre Jounel, Hans Urs von Balthasar, Louis Bouyer, A. M. Rouget, Joseph Gelineau, Francois Coudreau, Charles Moeller, Joseph Lecuyer, and Otto Spuelbeck. *The Liturgy and the Word of God: Third National Congress of the Centre de Pastorale Liturgique in Strasbourg (1958)*. Collegeville, Minnesota: The Liturgical Press, 1959.

Louf, André. *Teach Us to Pray*. Translated by Hubert Hoskins. London: Darton, Longman and Todd, 1974.

de Lubac, Henri. *Theological Fragments*. Translated by Rebecca Howell Balinski. San Francisco: Ignatius, 1989.

———. *Medieval Exegesis*. 2 vols. Translated by Marc Sebanc. Grand Rapids, Michigan: Eerdmans, 1998 (orig. 1959–1963).

———. *Corpus Mysticum: The Eucharist and the Church in the Middle Ages*. Translated by Gemma Simmonds et al. Notre Dame, Indiana: University of Notre Dame Press, 2006 (orig. 1949).

McAleer, G. J. *Ecstatic Morality and Sexual Politics: A Catholic and Antitotalitarian Theory of the Body*. New York: Fordham University Press, 2005.

Mansini, Guy. "On Affirming a Dominical Intention of a Male Priesthood." *The Thomist* 61/2 (1997), 301–16.

Margrassi, Mariano. *Praying the Bible: An Introduction to Lectio Divina*. Translated by Edward Hagman. Collegeville, Minnesota: Liturgical Press, 1998.

Maritain, Jacques. *Existence and the Existent*. Garden City, NY: Double-day, 1957.

Nédoncelle, Maurice. *The Personalist Challenge: Intersubjectivity and Ontology*. Translated by Francois C. Gérard and Francis F. Burch. Eugene, Oregon: Pickwick, 1984.

Norris, R.A. "The Ordination of Women and the 'Maleness' of Christ." *Supplementary Series of the Anglican Theological Review* 6 (June 1976), 69–80.

Nygren, Anders. *Agape and Eros*. Translated by Philip S. Watson. London: SPCK, 1953.

O'Neill, Colman E. *Meeting Christ in the Sacraments*. rev. ed. New York: Alba House, 1991.

O'Rourke, Fran. *Pseudo-Dionysius and the Metaphysics of Aquinas*. Notre Dame: University of Notre Dame Press, 2005.

Osborne, Catherine. *Eros Unveiled: Plato and the God of Love*. Oxford: Clarendon Press, 1994.

Ouellet, Marc. "Priestly ministry at the service of ecclesial communion." *Communio* 23 (1996), 677–87.

———. *Divine Likeness: Toward a Trinitarian Anthropology of the Family*. Translated by Philip Milligan and Linda M. Cicone. Grand Rapids: Eerdmans, 2006.

Perl, Eric D. "'Every Life is a Thought': the Analogy of Personhood in Neoplatonism." *Philosophy and Theology* 18/1 (2006), 143–67.

Peterson, Eugene. *Working the Angles: The Shape of Pastoral Integrity*. Grand Rapids: Eerdmans, 1987.

Pieper, Josef. *Problems of Modern Faith: Essays and Addresses*. Translated by Jan van Heurck. Chicago: Franciscan Herald Press, 1985.

———. *Living the Truth*. San Francisco: Ignatius, 1989.

———. *Divine Madness: Plato's Case against Secular Humanism*. Translated by Lothar Krauth. San Francisco: Ignatius, 1995.

———. *Faith, Hope, Love*. San Francisco: Ignatius, 1997.

Prétot, Patrick. "La Liturgie, Une Expérience Corporelle." *La Maison-Dieu* 247 (2006), 7–36.

Polanyi, Michael. "Faith and Reason." *Journal of Religion* 41/4 (1961), 237–47.

Quasten, Johannes. *Patrology*. vol. 1. Westminster: Newman Press, 1950.

Quay, Paul M. "Contraception and Conjugal Love." *Theological Studies* 22 (1961) 18–40.

Ratzinger, Joseph. *The Feast of Faith*. San Francisco: Ignatius, 1986.

————. *God is Near Us: The Eucharist, Heart of Life.* Translated by Henry Taylor. San Francisco: Ignatius, 2003.

————. *Pilgrim Fellowship of Faith: The Church as Communion.* Translated by Henry Taylor. San Francisco: Ignatius, 2005.

Rousselot, Pierre. *The Problem of Love in the Middle Ages: A Historical Contribution.* Translated by Alan Vincelette. Milwaukee: Marquette University Press, 2001 (orig. 1908).

Schindler, D.C. "The Redemption of Eros: Philosophical Reflections on Benedict XVI's First Encyclical." *Communio* 33 (2006), 375–99.

Schindler, David L. "The Person: Philosophy, Theology and Receptivity." *Communio* 21/1 (1994), 172–90.

Schlier, Heinrich. *The Relevance of the New Testament.* Translated by W. J. O'Hara. London: Burns and Oates, 1968.

Schloeder, Steven J. *Architecture in Communion: Implementing the Second Vatican Council through Liturgy and Architecture.* San Francisco: Ignatius, 1998.

Schmemann, Alexander. *Introduction to Liturgical Theology.* Translated by Asheleigh E. Moorhouse. New York: St. Vladimir's Seminary Press, 1996 (orig. 1975).

Schmitz, Kenneth L. *The Gift: Creation.* Milwaukee: Marquette University Press, 1982.

Scola, Angelo. *The Nuptial Mystery.* Translated by Michelle K. Borras. Grand Rapids: Eerdmans, 2005.

Sebanc, Marc. "J.R.R. Tolkien: Lover of the Logos." *Communio* 20 (1993) 84–106.

Soskice, Janet Martin. *Metaphor and Religious Language.* Oxford: Clarendon Press, 1987.

Spicq, Ceslaus. *Agape in the New Testament.* 3 vols. St. Louis and London: Herder, 1966.

Steinberg, Leo. "How Shall This Be? Reflections on Filippo Lippi's 'Annunciation' in London, Part I." *Artibus et Historiae* 8/16 (1987), 25–44.

Tolkien, J.R.R. *On Fairy-Stories.* Edited by Verlyn Flieger and Douglas A. Anderson. London: Harper Collins, 2008.

Wadell, Paul J. *The Primacy of Love: An Introduction to the Ethics of Thomas Aquinas.* New York/Mahwah: Paulist Press, 1992.

Weinrich, William. *It is not given to women to teach: A lex in search of a ratio.* Fort Wayne, Indiana: Concordia Theological Library Press, 1991.

Wilhelmsen, Frederick D. *The Metaphysics of Love.* London: Sheed and

Ward, 1962.

————. *The Paradoxical Structure of Existence.* Albany, NY: Preserving Christian Publications, 1991.

.

Index of Names

Index of Subjects

47–50, 62, 65–67, 78, 81, 83–84, 87, 91, 95–97

Marriage, ii, 2, 14, 33–34, 54, 62– 65, 67, 92, 97
  vows, 32–33, 97
  of Christ and Church, 6–8, 24, 29, 66–67, 80, 91, 93, 96–97
Mary (Theotokos), 35, 61, 75, 78–79
Matter, 14, 18, 50
Metaphysics, ii, 3, 7, 9–18, 23, 29, 36, 39, 43–44, 95–96
Monasticism, 72–73

Passover, 45–46, 83
Performativity, 6–7, 23, 31–35, 38–39, 43–46, 49, 65, 71, 80, 82, 84, 90, 95–97
Personhood, 10, 13, 15–16
Prayer, 4, 28, 38, 50, 65, 69–80, 86–87
Priest, 4, 28–29, 33, 35, 39, 55–67, 83, 85, 87, 90, 93
Priesthood, 37, 53, 56– 58, 61–62, 64, 66
Procreation, 34, 63
Prophetism, 7–8, 38, 95–97
Prophets, 2, 7, 46
Psalmody, 73

Reason, 5, 9, 40, 48, 53, 76
Receptivity, ii, 5, 7, 11–17, 29, 95
Relation, iii, 4, 10, 12–14, 16–18, 22, 50, 53, 58, 80, 95
Resurrection, 30, 34, 47, 55, 62–63, 67, 74, 77, 88–93, 97
Revelation, 8, 18, 21, 30, 58, 59, 92

Sacrifice, 28, 31, 34–35, 37, 56, 59, 66, 69, 81–88, 90, 92, 96
Scripture, 1, 5, 16, 30, 32, 44, 51, 54, 69, 71–74
Song of Songs, 21
Solitude, 14, 79
Suffering, 5, 7, 18–19, 22–25, 29, 49– 50, 81, 84, 86, 95–96

Temple (in Jerusalem), 35–36
Theologia, 3–4
Theologia prima (primary theology), iii, 5, 6, 7
Trinity, ii–iii, 3, 5, 17–18, 50, 53, 55, 58, 79, 86, 91, 97

Vatican II, 69
Virginity, 62–67

Women's ordination, 61

Made in the USA
Columbia, SC
23 January 2019